CHURCH HEALTH AND GROWTH PRIMER

Brad Miller

CHURCHTECH PRESS

www.churchtech.com

Church Health and Growth Primer

Copyright © 2010 The Rev. Dr. Bradley W. Miller. All rights reserved, including the right to reproduce this book or portions thereof in any form or by any means whatsoever. For information address:

ChurchTech Press
www.churchtech.com

Scripture quotations marked NLT are taken from the Holy Bible, New Living Translation, copyright 1996, 2004. Used by permission of Tyndale House Publishers, Inc., Wheaton, Illinois 60189. All rights reserved.

Quotations designated (NET) are from the NET Bible® copyright ©1996-2006 by Biblical Studies Press, L.L.C. www.bible.org All rights reserved. Scripture quoted by permission.

Scripture taken from the HOLY BIBLE, NEW INTERNATIONAL VERSION®. Copyright © 1973, 1978, 1984 Biblica. Used by permission of Zondervan. All rights reserved. The "NIV" and "New International Version" trademarks are registered in the United States Patent and Trademark Office by Biblica. Use of either trademark requires the permission of Biblica.

Scripture quotations marked MSG are taken from The Message. Copyright � 1993, 1994, 1995, 1996, 2000, 2001, 2002. Used by permission of NavPress Publishing Group.

Scripture quotations marked NASB are taken from the NEW AMERICAN STANDARD BIBLE®, Copyright © 1960,1962,1963,1968,1971,1972,1973, 1975,1977,1995 by The Lockman Foundation. Used by permission.

Scripture quotations marked NRSV are from New Revised Standard Version Bible, copyright © 1989 National Council of the Churches of Christ in the United States of America. Used by permission. All rights reserved

ISBN-13: 978-0-9823119-0-5

ISBN-10: 0-9823119-0-7

Manufactured in the U.S.A.

Dedication

To Emily and Byron, my children.

Acknowledgements

I am grateful for the support of many in helping this project come to fruition. Lyle Schaller's writing first inspired me to apply serious analytic tools to the work of ministry. His books and conferences have taught me more than I can describe.

Kent Hunter mentored me in the Church Doctor training process, gave me opportunities to consult through Church Doctor Ministries, and gave me the encouragement to develop my own consulting practice.

Merv Thompson mentored me in my church planting days and continues to help me process the examples of ministry excellence that arise at Lutheran Church of Hope and other places of church innovation.

All of the congregations that I have consulted and all those that I have served as pastor have shaped my understanding of church in a real world setting. Some times and places got a little too real, but I am grateful for the lessons that we learned together.

Pam Schroeder, my wife, is a wise pastor possessing all of the patience and pastoral attentiveness that I lack. Her love and prodding have supported me and made possible my travels, interim positions, and writing.

Table of Contents

		page
Prologue	....	1
Introduction	....	3
Church Growth Baggage	....	6
Body of Christ	....	10
Leadership	....	13
Gift Leverage	....	19
Governance	....	25
Worship	....	32
Small Groups	....	39
Worldview	....	43
Facilities	....	47
Location	....	55
Evangelism	....	60
Vision	....	69
Technology	....	73
Symbiosis	....	81
Programs	....	86
Leverage	....	88
Assessment	....	93
Money	....	99
Epilogue	....	104
About the Author	....	105

Prologue

The goals of this book are threefold, each matching a different meaning of the word "primer". First, is the sense of a book of basic instruction, as in the primers used as textbooks in schools, particularly in 19th century America. They did not contain lessons for mastering calculus or molecular biology, but rather they taught basic reading, writing, and arithmetic. Second, is the sort of primer that you might use when painting. It is not necessarily the texture, gloss, or color that you ultimately desire. But, it is a necessary base coat which prepares the surface for the ultimate finish that is intended. Third, is the type of primer that is used with explosives. Many types of explosive are quite stable most of the time – a good thing for those who handle and transport them. Some can be shaken, dropped, or even burned without catastrophic effect. An explosive primer, for instance a blasting cap, is a device which itself creates a small but intense burst of simultaneous heat and pressure which ignites some other explosive material into a large detonation.

This book will give you a basic understanding of church health and growth. It will do so in a manner which allows you to then build upon it through other reading, conferences, prayer, advice, and discernment. Finally, it will excite, inspire, and prod you to move forward with making your own church more effective in carrying out the unique plan that God has for it.

This book is not intended to function as a cookie-cutter to enable you to copy some other successful church and remake your own in that image. It is not a menu, giving you a list of programs that you can choose from based on what sounds most appealing or appetizing. And, it is certainly not an autobiography of success. In my 17 years of parish ministry I have served more churches that have resisted the principles that lead to growth than churches that have embraced such principles.

As I write this prologue, I am sitting in a small village in Mali, in West Africa. I am temporarily residing with a medical mission after a week of meetings about clean water projects and church planting methods. As the medical mission draws near an end, some of the supplies are dwindling. Difficult resource balancing decisions are made each evening about how, among the various clinics, to distribute the following day's limited supply of antibiotics, pain relievers, and anti-malarials. Most of the drugs are not, of course, interchangeable. Malaria medicine won't alleviate a backache. Aspirin won't fight an infection. Even the antibiotics themselves have differing degrees to which they are each effective for different infections. The right diagnosis and the right medicine are both essential for a good outcome.

In many parts of the world, we have pharmacies at which we can buy a wide range of medications. But some medicines require a prescription, either because of their potential danger or because they would be of little value without a doctor's diagnosis of the condition for which they are intended. Many years ago, my doctor once suggested that I take a common antihistamine for my allergies. It made me feel tired and did not stop my sneezing. I could decide from that experience that all doctors and all medicines are useless – but that would simply be silly. Ironically, many churches have been tricked into a comparably senseless conclusion. They have equated the bad experience with one "expert," or author, or program as a judgment against all knowledge and experience about church growth. This book is for those who want their church to be healthy and who are willing to learn, think, pray, and reflect in order to create the best opportunity for that health.

Introduction

In the summer of 2007 many baseball fans, both casual and committed, demonstrated a noteworthy level of indifference as Barry Bonds approached and then surpassed the Major League Baseball all time homerun record held for three decades by Hank Aaron. Why the ho-hum response to breaking such a famous record? Most attributed the disinterest to the widespread presumption that Bonds had used steroids to build the muscles with which he swung the bat so effectively. At the same time, Floyd Landis was mounting a very public defense of his year earlier Tour de France win – an honor which had been stripped from him based on a urinalysis test indicating the use of forbidden performance enhancing substances.

And yet, simultaneously, hundreds of thousands of amateur athletes were training through individually unique regimens of exercise, weightlifting, diet, and practice in their chosen sport. Did they give up because they were disappointed in Barry Bonds and Floyd Landis? Of course not! Most understood that the use of potentially dangerous steroids were an aberration or an extreme misapplication of the personal fitness goals that they were pursuing.

Would some percentage of athletes follow the example of Bonds hoping that they, too, could avail themselves of the seemingly fantastic shortcut to the kind of body they seek? Sure, some people will always take shortcuts, however risky they might prove to be. Instant gratification in bodybuilding, we now know, is just as dangerous as the instant gratification in consumer goods that has caused an explosion in consumer debt, a housing market crisis, and created a virtual debtor nation within American society.

Also during the summer of 2007, attention continued to grow towards a rising concern in America – that of obesity, particularly childhood obesity. A growing chorus of health experts began to raise the possibility that we could actually see a generational decline in life expectancy because of the increased morbidity arising from cardiac disease, diabetes, and cancer among the obese.

If your child were dangerously overweight and had no physical stamina, would you say to yourself: "I am so relieved that my kid is not abusing steroids." I doubt it. You understand that steroid induced super-muscles and morbid obesity are not an either/or choice. Rather, each is an unhealthy extreme – seeming opposites on a continuum. In reality there is not a linear continuum, because there are other unhealthy body profiles – like anorexia – that are quite different. In the middle of those diverse but equally unhealthy choices lie a broad range of relatively healthy body styles. That healthy middle is where we all want to be. Genetics, willpower, stress, environment, conscious choices, and other factors all influence how close to the middle we land (or stay).

Building a healthy body is definitely a good thing. We can debate about how much sacrifice it is worth. We can differ about ideal weights and shapes. Good and bad cholesterol levels may be continually redefined by specialists in the field. We can argue about the effectiveness of different diet plans. You may prefer free weights over the computerized resistance machines at the fitness center. But, despite all of those differences, assuredly we can agree that a strong, healthy body is a good and desirable thing.

What did St. Paul call the Church in I Corinthians 12 and likewise in Ephesians? He called the Church the *Body of Christ*. The fact that we should be attentive to the healthy growth of that body should not be controversial. Of course agreement on this point won't end feuds within Christendom. We may still argue about when to baptize, how literally to interpret which portions of scripture, whether wine or grape juice should be used for communion, and a dozen other topics.

Starting to agree broadly that Jesus wasn't just joking when he proclaimed the Great Commission (Matthew 28:16-20) has several noteworthy benefits:

- First, it honors God and God's holy word.

- Second, it removes one source of needless division within the Body of Christ.
- Third, it lets us learn from apparent ministry failures and successes rather than wasting the occasions with disparaging or triumphal blaming.
- Fourth, it lets us begin to engage in honest, healthy, constructive discussions about individual congregational growth strategies.

Some ventures implemented in the name of church growth have been ineffective, like some of the over-the-counter herbal health remedies which have no effect. Some ventures have been carried out primarily due to human ego, like a teenage girl recklessly starving herself to match the image of an emaciated supermodel. Some ventures have reflected toxic distortions of the Gospel, like the athletes who have disregarded societal laws and rules of their own sports by using banned steroids. Some ventures have been solid ideas implemented at the wrong time or place, like a person taking a properly prescribed cholesterol-lowering statin drug while maintaining the seemingly healthy habit of eating fresh grapefruit for breakfast. (In case you haven't heard, good ole healthy grapefruit negates the benefits of such drugs and can even cause harm.)

In our rapidly changing modern medical world, we each need to be smart consumers. We need to take responsibility for our own health care and stay informed about what tests we need, what the results may mean, and what the benefits and dangers may be for various treatment plans. We want to make informed and rational decisions. We don't want to ignore potentially lifesaving treatments just because someone else had one bad experience with a similar treatment. Our churches need leaders who are equally discerning about the range of options for encouraging the health and growth of our congregations.

Church Growth Baggage

Have you noticed the format that 24 hour cable news channels have migrated to for dealing with topics? They tend to simultaneously interview two "experts" that take opposite sides of whatever issue is being discussed. Sometimes the "experts" reputations are widely known – but sometimes not. There are a growing number of people who are making a career as professional naysayers. News producers know that if they need a quote against topic "X", they can just spin their Rolodex (or computer contact manager) to a preferred "anti-X expert".

In reality, this phenomenon precedes television. Especially in the church, there is a long pattern of careers founded upon being vocally against something: a worship style, a new Bible translation, a political issue, a denominational office. More than a few pastors, bishops, authors, and seminary presidents have found a path to success in being vocally against something. Of course (presuming statistically that *any* issue can be divided into pro and con) half the time the opposition may be right. Each of us has a mix of views in the broad range of life issues. It is natural for us to favor some ideas and oppose others. Certainly nothing is wrong with that. Even the original disciples could disagree, as at the Council of Jerusalem in Acts 15. The problem is that we need to be aware that some people have a deeply vested interest in fanning opposition to a concept, idea, or movement - and their motivation may be more inspired by practical personal benefit than by deeply held principle.

There are four key reasons why people have become opposed to Church Growth. First is the quite small but significant category of folks who are anti-Church Growth because that opposition has, crassly, been a boon to their careers. This is the smallest and the loudest group. Second are the folks who have equated all Church Growth with a few practices or personalities that they dislike. Many of these folks believe in the Great Commission, but have come to view Church Growth as a lumped together category of all the wrong ways to make disciples. Third, is the large number of people whose worldview does not embrace the

Great Commission as an essential part of Christianity. They see fellowship, or social advocacy, or moral teaching, or worship, or something else, as the predominant purpose of the church - to the exclusion of evangelism and disciplemaking. Fourth, are the vary large group composed of those who have trusted the biased view of someone from one of the three groups above and accepted that judgment without further research.

Church Growth is not a protected brand name, so anyone can use the phrase. It came into common usage in a time of social and spiritual turbulence. The birth control pill, the drug culture, the civil rights movement, Vatican II, the Berlin Wall, the Vietnam War, the Beatles, integrated circuits, assassinations, ecumenism, color TV, and the Church Growth movement all burst into our culture at about the same time. Our hopes, fears, and biases about all of those diverse topics became entangled with our first impressions of church growth. (Editors Note: in deference to the reality that it is not a proper noun with any clearly agreed sense of identity, we are dropping the capitalization from this point forward.) If Fuller Seminary had been in Nebraska, rather than California, early responses to church growth might have been very different. Hollywood, Haight-Ashbury hippies, the Watts Riots, and the Manson Family all made it too easy to treat anything coming from California with suspicion.

For some, this movement was threatening because it was part of a new wave of churches looking beyond the narrow confines of their denomination for resources and advice. Some people associated it with charismatic worship because *some* church growth practitioners were charismatic and that topic was very divisive in certain circles. Some people associated it with TV evangelists and questionable fundraising methods. Some people associated it with slick suits (replacing liturgical vestments) and later, even Hawaiian shirts!

There is no official church growth dress code, or interpretation of Genesis, or acceptance of speaking in tongues. The movement was the logical outcome of growth in the fields of research and sociology during and after WWII. Sooner or later, someone was going to apply tools like surveys, observation, and statistical analysis to the work of the church in response to the Great Commission. We are blessed that it happened. Once the insights from such research were released, leaders took that knowledge and ran with it in all sorts of different directions. Those using this knowledge spanned the ranges of liberal and conservative, selfish and selfless, wise and foolish.

Some people kept observing what seemed to be working and tried to figure out why. Successes and failures were considered. The definitions of success and failure were considered and reconsidered. In seminaries, para-church organizations, and denominational offices, that work continues today.

The fear of big was another important social force concurrent with the church growth movement. Various states were forcing small school districts to merge. Small downtown shops started to be replaced by large suburban malls. Small hospitals were being replaced by large ones. People saw large institutions as a threat to small ones. If church growth was going to produce larger churches, it would be hitting another cultural raw nerve.

Perhaps the most cited concern was the perception that the church growth movement was "only about numbers." Numbers do play a significant role in research and statistical analysis. In order to objectively observe trends and patterns, you need to find things that are measurable, like: number of members, number of people in attendance, or number of dollars given. These things can seem superficial, even trivial, given the unique burdens and blessings that ministry encompasses. How can the aftermath of a suicide be reduced to a number? How can a baptism be reduced to a number?

It is good that people realize that ministry is more than mere numbers. Have you ever driven on an interstate highway as part of a family vacation? Did you notice mile marker signs on the roadside? Did you realize that the exits are usually numbered to match those numbers? They make navigating easier. If you have a flat tire, the towing company will ask what mile marker you are closest to. You probably didn't take a picture with your family grouped around a mile marker. The mile markers could never replace your memories of what was funny or surprising or disappointing. But those mile markers would clearly chart a record of where you had been.

Numbers are used throughout the Bible. Remember, there is even an entire book named Numbers! Numbers can never replace people and relationships – and we wouldn't want them to. Numbers, like interstate mile markers, are simply tools to help us stay on course and measure our progress.

Church growth isn't about the preacher's choice of shirt, or the tempo of music, or about just having more members and more money. Churches grow as a natural outcome of being healthy and heeding the Great Commission. Systematically paying attention to what works and what doesn't work could be called church growth, or it could just be called common sense. The label doesn't matter. Ministry matters.

Body of Christ

Just as our bodies have many parts and each part has a special function, so it is with Christ's body. We are many parts of one body, and we all belong to each other.

– Romans 12:4-5 (NLT)

If you've been around the church long, then you've assuredly heard sermons about the Body of Christ. All Christians together make up that body. Individual congregations are both a part of that whole body and also a miniature expression of it. The reality that we are the Body of Christ has profound implications which should shape our whole approach to how we live, work, and make decisions together as congregations.

Have you ever been a member of a non-church club? I am a Rotarian. Once a week I get together for one hour with other Rotarians. We visit, eat, sing a song, and listen to a speaker. Many of my friends are Rotarians. If I am out of town, I can make-up my missed meeting at a Rotary Club anyplace around the world. Through Rotary, I've participated in local projects for youth, fundraisers for worthy causes, and traveled to Africa working on a clean water project. Rotary, like many other clubs, makes the world a better place. But, Rotary is not a church. To start, Rotary is not concerned with eternal matters. But much more importantly, Christ makes no claim to it. Christ clearly claims the church as expressed through Paul's teaching and in Jesus' own words in John 15 that: *I am the vine; you are the branches.*

This critical difference shapes the mission, vision, and values of every healthy church. If your church leadership does not have crystal clarity about this unique nature, then none of the chapters which follow will matter much. The Body of Christ has resources that no club could imagine and eternal responsibilities that no club would want.

The most legitimate concern about church growth is when good principles are misused by clubs pretending to be churches. Sometimes this happens through the overt fraud of self-interested leaders. More often it happens through collective denial as what was once a church morphs slowly into an institution more interested in the comfort of those who are already members than in the needs of the world around them.

Assuring that your church remains rooted in Christ is a task that precedes, accompanies and follows each of the topics which follow. So please remember that...

...you must lead consistent with Christ's teaching.
...gifts must be leveraged for the sake of Christ's mission.
...your governance is for the Body of Christ, not a club.
...God (Father, Son, and Holy Spirit) is who we worship.
...small groups nurture our faith in Christ.
...we are called to view the world as Christ does.
...it is God's building that we use and take care of.
...our location is a tiny spot in God's creation.
...we evangelize by Christ's command.
...it is God's vision entrusted to us.
...technological tools are useful when in service to God.

What follows will help your church function better. Always remember *why* you function when you contemplate *how* you function. Remember also that other churches are part of the same Body of Christ. The only competition that we really face is that of the world and the devil. Winning and losing in ministry is measured by souls in eternity. Winning and losing with those consequences is far too serious to be treated like a game.

Leadership

Choose for each of your tribes individuals who are wise, discerning, and reputable to be your leaders.

- *Deuteronomy 1:13 (NRSV)*

Churches are not exactly tribes, but they still need leaders. Congregation size and governance style profoundly shape the roles of leaders. You may be considered a leader because you were elected or appointed to a particular position. You may be a leader because, regardless of office or position, people look to you when decisions are made. Whatever the scope or origin of your authority, leading well honors God and serves your congregation.

The above passage from Deuteronomy gives us a good starting point to consider this topic. It could be phrased another way: seek to apply wisdom and discernment to your tasks while retaining the trust of the congregation. Wisdom is related to, but not synonymous with, knowledge. Even full-time clergy with advanced degrees who intentionally participate in a range of Continuing Education opportunities, can not be expert in all ministry topics. Part of being wise is recognizing the limits of our knowledge. We serve our congregation well when we acknowledge that we are simply unable to know it all. Equipped with that insight, we quest to learn more about our area of ministry. We also seek the input of those who've worked in that area, both in our congregation and in other places.

Full recognition of how little we know can yield a dangerous by-product: analysis paralysis. We can become so focused on getting more information that we never progress to using that information. Balancing the known and the unknown is a key part of discernment. Discerning can be narrowly defined as perceiving God's will. More broadly though, it entails not just what God wants us to do, but also when and how. Discernment without prayer and the guidance of scripture is merely the identification of a human preference.

Being a reputable leader means being a trusted leader. Trust is earned, not granted. Trust is far easier to lose than it is to gain. Betrayal of trust in any one area of our lives can lead to a loss of trust in all others. It is logical that abuse of trust leads to loss of trust, but the ability to trust is not purely rational. My Border Collie doesn't trust any tall men. We can only surmise that, before we adopted him from the animal shelter, he had some bad experience with a tall man. People are both smarter and more complicated than dogs. Someone in your church may not trust you because your hair style, vocation, vocal pitch, or shirt color reminds them of someone that once betrayed their trust. That hindrance is neither rational nor fair, but effective leaders seek ways to demonstrate that they are trustworthy.

Trust is especially difficult to maintain without clarity of purpose and good communications. If your church functions as a loose confederation of programs, then cutting funds to one program while adding to another may well be seen as a betrayal by the fans of the cut program – unless that decision is communicated in a way that demonstrates its strategic value in furtherance of broader goals. If the congregation doesn't have a shared sense of a clear future direction, then leading becomes much more difficult. Trust maintenance through ongoing and effective communications is especially important because churches frequently deal with confidential matters that can't be disclosed. In those situations, a leader's only option is to draw on the bank of trust that they have steadily been making deposits into.

It is a mistake to presume that being trusted is the same as being popular. Doing the right thing won't always get you invited to the cool party – ask any teenager! It is not uncommon for a leader, in any setting, to discover that wisdom and discernment point in a direction that would not be popular with the broader group. Those are the occasions that require us to live up to our title and do what leaders are required to do: **lead**.

Leading isn't just figuring out what other people want, though good leaders avail themselves of that information. Leading isn't just approving minutes and financial reports, though leaders do care about such things. Leading isn't just about advocating for a particular group, ministry, or program – though leaders have empathy and appreciation for those with such zeal. The process of leading can be summarized by the eight D's:

- **Deduce**: Analyze the problem, opportunity, or situation using your knowledge and the knowledge of others inside and outside your congregation.
- **Discern**: Through prayer and contemplation of scripture, seek God's guidance.
- **Decide**: Choose a course of action and develop a plan for implementing it.
- **Disseminate**: Communicate to the congregation what will be done, why it is being doing, and how it will be done.
- **Delegate**: Enlist assistance to accomplish the various tasks that comprise the plan.
- **Do**: Implement the plan.
- **Debrief**: Assess progress; learn from mistakes; listen to feedback.
- **Disciple**: Show and teach the next round of leaders what God has done and how God has used leaders in your congregation to accomplish it.

Leaders attend to the eight D's in a continuous and overlapping loop. Though the steps are sequential, they don't have rigid boundaries. For example, disseminating information and discipling do not stop merely because the next step has begun. The duration and detail of each step is appropriately scaled to the issue at hand: launching a new satellite ministry will take more time and effort than replacing the photocopier will.

On paper, leading looks easy. Out in the real world, opinions, attitudes, emotions, and personalities can all collide in ways that look more like a car wreck than a productive process. At such times, leaders need to draw on the counsel of Colossians 3:12-17 where Paul writes:

Therefore, as God's chosen people, holy and dearly loved, clothe yourselves with compassion, kindness, humility, gentleness and patience. Bear with each other and forgive whatever grievances you may have against one another. Forgive as the Lord forgave you. And over all these virtues put on love, which binds them all together in perfect unity.

Let the peace of Christ rule in your hearts, since as members of one body you were called to peace. And be thankful. Let the word of Christ dwell in you richly as you teach and admonish one another with all wisdom, and as you sing psalms, hymns and spiritual songs with gratitude in your hearts to God. And whatever you do, whether in word or deed, do it all in the name of the Lord Jesus, giving thanks to God the Father through him. (NIV)

So, how do leaders stick to Paul's advice once the name-calling starts? It is hard. The critical starting point is for leaders to be spiritually healthy before and during the time of leadership service. Committed habits of daily prayer and scripture reading won't guarantee either a healthy Christian life or good Christian leadership, but they are the best possible foundation to start from. There is a strong correlation between spiritually healthy leaders and thriving congregations. Plus, Christians who are spiritually healthy before and during a tenure of service tend to remain healthy afterward. Far too many congregational leaders have drifted away from church because they suffered burn-out while serving.

Effective 8D leadership requires partnership among the different kinds of leaders in a congregation. Team is the theme. People with different gifts work toward shared goals. Whether the system is hierarchical or not, there is mutual accountability among all.

Those who volunteer to serve out of a motivation to control won't fit comfortably in such an environment. They will need to learn new skills and attitudes or find different ways to serve. I once arrived at a congregation in the final phases of the pastor's terminal illness. It had been that pastor's first ministerial posting. I was greeted on my first day in the office by a member of the congregation who explained that he was there to plan my schedule for the week. I was a bit surprised. He explained that in the time since he had retired two years before, he had managed the pastor's schedule each week. He told the pastor which meetings to attend (and which to skip) and which members to visit. He had run a large beverage distribution business and was accustomed to being in charge. So, as his retirement "hobby" he decided to run the pastor and the church. I politely declined his offer.

Because churches are dependent upon volunteers for so many essential functions, the risk is grave when volunteers are permitted to do what they want without boundaries. A group of leaders jointly seeking to know and do God's will embody healthy 8D leadership. A group of individuals each seeking to do whatever they want is no leadership at all.

Years later, that same church with the calendar control issues had made great progress. They were using the first seven D's quite well. After decades of vision paralysis they had pulled together and made great strides forward. They had built a new facility and ramped up to the start of an additional worship service. Then, two church council members received job transfers out of state, one had a health crisis, and two more saw their elected terms expire. Virtually overnight they went from being a cohesive leadership team to a collection of individuals with separate agendas. To use a sports metaphor, I had neglected to develop our "bench" – our reserve leaders who would be ready to step up and lead when needed. That was when I added the eighth D, discipling. Whatever else is happening, churches need to be constantly equipping the next round of leaders.

Of course, not all church leaders are volunteers. Paid church professionals are part of the congregational leadership mix. Like a good rowing team, staff and volunteers must function as a cooperative team – otherwise, rather than progress toward a goal there is just a lot of thrashing of water.

A core issue to evolve in recent decades is a simple question with profound implications: should a pastor be a leader? A mindset has developed among some clergy and laity (non-clergy) that pastors ought to not intervene in important decisions. So, if a congregation were considering relocating or realigning denominational ties, the pastor would take no position on the matter. This deferential attitude is consistent with a ministry model popularized at many seminaries starting in the 1950's and 1960's. This model treats pastoral social work done by the pastor on behalf of the congregation as the core function of pastors. Many good and faithful pastors have served full careers with this approach.

Unfortunately, it isn't a very good model for ministry. It encourages a proxy Christian mindset that negates the spiritual gifts for care ministries of many non-pastors. It doesn't follow Christ's example of training, multiplying, and releasing followers to serve. It encourages congregations to avoid growth, so that they can stay at a comfortable size able to be served by one pastor. Finally, there just aren't many good examples from scripture, church history, or organizational theory in businesses and non-profits to support the notion of the most visible personal presence in an organization being mute on the matters of greatest significance. Pastors should be leaders.

So, are you ready to become a better leader? There are virtually innumerable resources available to help you learn more about leadership. Not all are consistent with biblical principles. I recommend:

- Attending a Willow Creek Association Summit;
- Participating in one of John Maxwell's Leadership training programs;
- Reading one or more of Ken Blanchard's recent books which integrate management principles and Christian insights.

Gift Leverage

Now, dear brothers and sisters, regarding your question about the special abilities the Spirit gives us. I don't want you to misunderstand this.

- 1 Corinthians 12:1 (NLT)

Church buildings often incorporate art and architecture in ways that tell parts of our shared story of faith. Did you ever pause to realize that *how* the buildings are constructed also offer us important lessons? Builders combine the power of machines, the skills of people, and the properties of materials to create a finished structure. Plumbers use special tools to cut and bend pipe. HVAC specialists use different tools to cut and bend the ductwork for heating and air conditioning systems.

Builders have used machines for thousands of years – dating back even earlier than the construction of the pyramids in Egypt. Simple machines, like the pulley, lever, and screw, were used then and are still used today. Simple machines use leverage to multiply force. The right tools make the job easier and the finished product better. Using the right people for the right jobs is another kind of leverage.

Imagine that you are the contractor for a large building project. One day, you decide to add some excitement by shuffling up the work assignments. The plumbers are sent to do framing work. The framers are sent to do wiring. The electricians are sent to do accounting. The accountants are sent to lay carpet. The carpet layers are told to create building plans. The architects are sent to install shingles. The roofers are sent to do plumbing. It might all be interesting for a day. It would also be dangerous and inefficient in the long run. Some of the employees could be retrained, but training alone can't offset the reality that some people simply have innate, god-gifted aptitudes for certain kinds of tasks.

No contractor would run a business this way. Sadly, many churches function (or dysfunction) in a manner not terribly different. Sam was a very talented member who contributed many hours serving in many ways at a church I once served. Sam took a recurring spot in the rotating schedule of greeters who welcomed visitors and members to church on Sunday mornings. Unfortunately, Sam was germophobic and had a generally unpleasant demeanor. So, the first interaction of many visitors to our church was with a person who was grim, unsmiling, and refused to shake a hand. Sam was still a great person loved by God, but the church was utilizing Sam in a manner contrary to the gifts that God had given – to the detriment of the congregation.

There are four key scripture passages that are traditionally looked to for guidance about spiritual gifts:
- 1 Corinthians chapters 12-14
- Romans chapter 12
- Ephesians chapter 4
- 1 Peter chapter 4

Each has great value. Integrating the guidance from these four very different New Testament writings is challenging because it cuts across two of the most emotionally charged and divisive lightening rods of the modern church: Cessationism and Biblical Literalism. Embracing the importance of Spiritual Gifts need not wait for agreement on the other matters, but a brief overview may be helpful.

Cessationism is the view that certain gifts ceased to be given by the Holy Spirit at some time in the historic past, generally coinciding with the end of the New Testament. The gifts that are argued to have ceased generally include Tongues, Prophecy, and Apostleship. The complete opposite view is that those same gifts are not only present today, but also indicative of whether a person is genuinely Christian. In between those polar opposites are many subtlely distinctive positions regarding the dates, reasons, and particular gifts that were ceased and/or resumed. In the middle are a broad group of Christians who make no claim to possess "ceased" gifts, but also refrain from disputing that others today may possess such gifts. There are vibrant, faithful, growing churches all across this spectrum. The critical commonality that they share is a commitment to teach and encourage the use of whatever gifts they acknowledge.

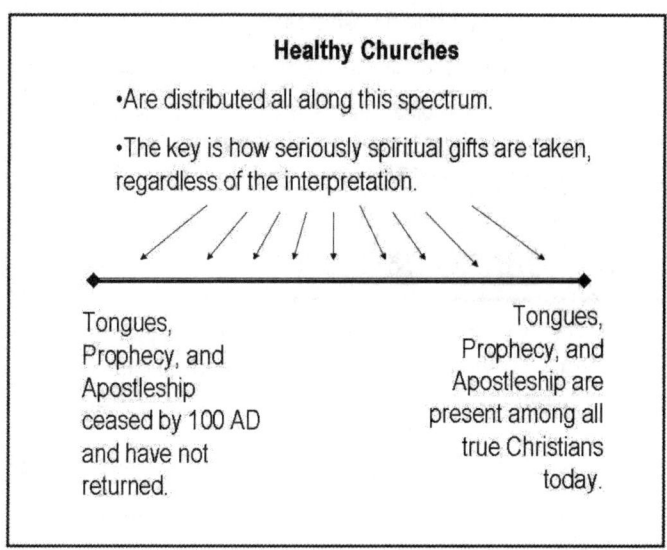

Biblical literalism is often mistakenly thought to be a binary state. In reality, like cessationism, there are a range of degrees of literalism. At one extreme are those who won't consider any source beyond the King James Version of the Bible. At the opposite extreme are those that see all of scripture as informative allegory, but no more *true* than ancient texts of other religions. In between are many points of view. Unlike the cessationism continuum, vibrant, faithful, growing churches tend to be clustered in a particular segment of this diversity. Healthy churches place a high value on scripture – though they may argue passionately about what constitutes *literal* or *inerrant*. Healthy churches tend to acknowledge the complexity of perfectly rendering Old Testament Hebrew and New Testament Greek into modern languages. They also acknowledge that tiny textual variants complicate the task of agreeing what words were originally inspired in particular passages. And, they realize that the presence or absence of a comma in Ephesians 4:12 has great importance in interpreting fivefold ministry. Healthy churches see these challenges as an invitation to study, not as an excuse to minimize the importance of scripture.

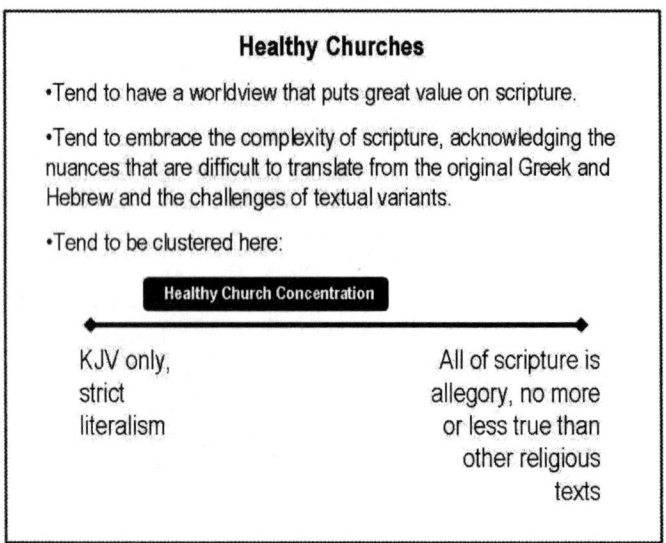

How a church views cessation will, clearly, have an effect on how it counsels and encourages members to use certain gifts. How a church interprets scripture has great bearing on how the teachings of 1st Corinthians, Romans, Ephesians, and 1st Peter are reconciled. The essential truth is that your congregation needs to fully utilize Spiritual Gifts in whatever way is most consistent with your doctrine – knowing that ignoring these teachings can't be justified by any Christian doctrine!

There is one dangerous misconception which particularly merits addressing. If you read the scripture passages listed above, you will note a glaring omission. There is no mention of *Pastor as Super-Christian*. It is an imaginary and unscriptural concept, though quite commonly presumed to exist. We expect pastors to be competent in a wide range of functions. We slip into quicksand when we fail to differentiate between competence and gifting. If a pastor is great at preaching and visitation, do we still expect that pastor to be the primary teacher – even if he or she is not particularly good at it?

I once served a church where the pastor was expected to teach confirmation classes (an overview of scripture and Luther's Catechism for Junior High students). I had taught such classes at other churches and was quite competent to do so, though not particularly gifted. After awhile, I discovered a layperson, Bob, who loved teaching youth. After a transition, Bob started to teach the class. The young people loved Bob, they learned more, they grew more in their faith, and they invited their friends. Confirmation class became a point of entry to our church. Then, at an annual congregational meeting, someone (with no children of the requisite age) attacked the program – and the people in it – because it wasn't being taught by a pastor. Soon after, I left to start a mission congregation in another city and Bob left for a church where his gifts were permitted to be used. The confirmation program shriveled up when the person with both gifts and passion for that ministry was gone.

In many churches, it is easier to have the pastor do a wide range of varied ministries than to find people with gifts in those areas. Easier, yes. Better, no. A few building contractors can design a house, frame it, wire it, plumb it, roof it, carpet it, drywall it, paint it, and install the furnace. The fact that they can do those things, doesn't mean that they can do each of them well. If your goal is to have a pastor be marginally competent in all areas of ministry, then you are sacrificing excellence in most of those areas. Wisely using the spiritual gifts of all members and staff is a point of leverage to enable more and better ministry.

It is imperative that churches do three things with regard to Spiritual Gifts:
- Teach all members about the different gifts.
- Provide all members with assessment tools to help identify the particular gifts of each member.
- Utilize members according to their gifts.

How familiar are you with your spiritual gifts? Talk with your pastor about a Spiritual Gifts Inventory that fits well with your congregation's understanding of gifts. I also recommend:

- Gilbert, Larry. <u>Team Ministry: How to Find Meaning and Fulfillment through Understanding the Spiritual Gifts within You</u>. Annapolis: Church Growth Institute, 1991.
- <u>The Biblical Personal Profile</u>, with assorted supporting materials based on the DiSC profile.
- Mallon, Paddy. <u>Calling A City Back To God</u>. Kingsway, 2003.

Governance

I may seem to be boasting too much about the authority given to us by the Lord. But this authority is to build you up, not to tear you down. And I will not be put to shame by having my work among you destroyed.

2 Corinthians 10:8 (NLT)

In the passage above, Paul both claims his authority and sets limits to it. Building up rather than tearing down, is a powerful frame in which to think about the governing of our churches. It rules out any selfish power grabs or mean-spirited attacks, while still leaving room for firm and principled disagreement. How many churches have been cursed by mean and petty conflicts that made no contribution to building up the congregation?

Governance and leadership are closely linked. If leadership were a paintbrush, then governance could be a medium to paint on. An artist would use different brushes and techniques for a mosaic on a brick wall, a portrait canvas, or a glossy sheet of 8 x 10 inch finger-paint paper. Leadership is about style and finesse. Governance is about structures and systems. Neither works without the other.

Scripture gifts us with a broad range of vocabulary and models for structuring decision-making in churches. Your governing board may use one or more names like: council, deacon, elder, trustee, committee, or vestry. Some forms of polity are required by certain denominations. Some forms work well with a particular church size, but are cumbersome and ineffective when the church gets either larger or smaller.

Whatever you call the decision-making leadership group in your church and however its rules are structured, that information should be contained in your governing documents. Typically these include a constitution and bylaws, but they may also be supported by continuing resolutions, council minutes, or policy documents. If you are a leader, it is important that you are familiar with these documents. You, individually, and your congregation can be put at legal risk if the rules and procedures specified by these documents are not followed.

How could these documents ever present such danger? Consider these scenarios, each of which could create legal jeopardy for your church if you have not adhered to its governing rules:

- **A wrongful termination lawsuit**: Your governing documents may indicate specific procedures for hiring and firing, especially for a pastor.
- **A schism within your church**: Your governing documents may dictate who retains ownership of the property.
- **Separation from your denomination**: Your governing documents may establish a process that must be followed.
- **Surety Bond**: If your governing documents describe a process for cash handling and audits, the protection of your bond could be cancelled if you don't follow those procedures.

More important even than avoiding legal exposure, the best reasons for governing document compliance are that they should make your life easier and your church healthier. Your life is easier because you are not spending energy constantly reinventing the wheel. Your church is healthier because good leaders incorporate the lessons learned from their experience and that of other churches into those important documents. They protect against pitfalls that others have faced. They provide sufficient flexibility to respond to new challenges and opportunities.

If your governing documents don't accomplish those purposes, then change them. If your governing documents don't match the way that you actually function, then change one to match the other. Preferably, you will pick what works best for your church as both the written policy and the actual practice. If you are substantially out of compliance, then you will need to create a plan to move to compliance over a period of time.

Is it possible to go overboard with all of this governing document stuff? Certainly! If everyone brings their constitution to the congregational meeting, but no one brings a Bible – that is a sure danger sign. People can obsess over procedure to the exclusion of ever dealing with substance.

Well constructed governing documents have a hierarchy among those documents. Typically the constitution contains the most fundamental doctrinal and procedural rules. Constitutional amendments tend to require a super-majority vote of the whole congregation with advance notice requirements. The bylaws contain more detail and are less cumbersome to amend. Policies or continuing resolutions are the most detailed and can typically be enacted by the governing board without a congregational meeting. Scaling the documents based on importance and level of detail provides, structure, safety, and flexibility, with each in proper measure.

When my children were toddlers, they had sets of nesting shapes among their toys. Several round cylinders could be stacked up in order with the largest cylinder at the bottom. They could also be nested, again requiring a proper order. There were square shapes, triangular shapes, and star shapes in sets as well. The differing shapes, of course, did not readily stack or nest with each other. Think of your governing documents as a set of nesting cubes. They fit inside one another in a particular order. They must be the same shape in order to nest. Your governing documents should all reflect a common philosophy about church governance. That philosophy should incorporate your understandings about authority, representation, polity, and membership.

Use your favorite Bible Search application to find references to "vote", "voted", and voting" in the Old and New Testaments. You may be surprised. Depending upon your chosen translation, your search may yield no occurrences at all. At most, you may find just a few. Democracy is not scripturally assumed as the foundational model of the church. Realistically, most churches in the USA are democratically organized to the extent that anyone denied a vote by ballot or show of hands retains the option to vote with their feet – and find a new church. Particularly with the erosion of denominational loyalty in recent decades, this phenomenon of choice seems here to stay. Still, who gets to vote and which matters require a vote is a core feature that makes your church distinctive in the wide range of church governance systems.

Democracy is not magical, but neither is it incompatible with good church governance. Pure democracy is a rarity reserved for very small groups. In a pure democracy, all decisions require a vote from everyone. There are a few obvious drawbacks to this arrangement. First, everyone has to be available whenever a decision needs to be made. Second, there is no practical way to delegate leadership tasks – so everyone needs to meet with all of the insurance sales representatives and all of the copier sales representatives in order to make an informed decision about those purchase decisions. Most of us are accustomed to some form of representative democracy. Representative democracy reserves some decisions for the entire collected group, but entrusts most decisions to a small selected group. Two classic challenges are presented by this modified option. First is the procedural question: how much authority does the small group have to make decisions without the approval of the large group? Second is the philosophical question: are the members of the small group expected use their own best judgment or are they expected to do what they think would be least upsetting to the large group?

Because leadership and governance are so closely linked, it is important to acknowledge that sometimes the unwritten rules of delegated decision-making authority change and no one notices until they have stepped over the new imaginary line. The church council (or comparable group) may have explicit authority to spend up to a set dollar amount or a set percentage of the adopted budgeted. They might choose to spend an amount well within that limit to replace worn carpet. They might then discover that carpet color is such a contentious issue that everyone wanted to have input. Leaders need to be continually reassessing how short a leash the congregation perceives itself to have granted. Mostly, this is a matter of earned trust. Emotional issues, however, can quickly evaporate the reserve of trust.

As you seek to devise a plan for governing your church, you will want to be aware of those dynamics we've already discussed. Many textbooks from the fields of political science or governance can shed light on the challenges of representative democracy. Churches are not, as you well know, counties, or states, or clubs. Hence, be sure that the following are also part of your governing system:

- **Strategic**: Incorporate a bias toward future planning and preparedness. Be sure that your system is not so overwhelmed by the *urgent* matters that it is perpetually delaying attention to the *important* matters. Make certain that some accountable person or group plays the critical role of seeing that all of the various ministries at your church are coordinated and focused on common goals.
- **Principled**: Observers should not be left to wonder if decisions are driven simply by expediency, popularity, or convenience. Your shared understanding of the purpose of the church should under-gird every aspect of your governing structure.
- **Faith-driven**: A church is not a club that merely happens to do religious stuff. Being the Body of Christ takes precedence over any other legal, organizational, or procedural principle.

Church leaders, when devising or adapting systems of governance, should give attention to the power of AND over OR, as well as the seemingly contradictory power of OR over AND. These concepts apply both in how we lead and in how we structure for decision-making. Recently, many churches have discovered the relative ease of creating an electronic version of the traditional newsletter. Armed with that knowledge, some have considered ending the print version. Making both versions available, at least for a substantial period of assessment, is a better option in most places. Giving people choices (AND) is generally better received than choosing for them (OR). Sometimes though, churches find that they have accumulated a glut of programmatic options and that reducing many options down to a few is a means to channel time and other resources more effectively. Strategic thinking sometimes requires tough choices (OR) so that a wide variety of under-supported programs (AND) don't function like weeds choking out ministry priorities.

Often, the dysfunctions of our system become so familiar to us that we fail to recognize either the harms that they cause or the opportunities that they preclude us from exploring. Sometimes an outsider brings the perspective that helps us better understand our context. In the aftermath of Enron and other corporate frauds, Sarbanes-Oxley became law in the United States. One element of this new regulatory requirement has been the expanded practice of *outside directors*. Outside directors are presumed to fulfill the role of unbiased truth teller. Whether through the work of a consultant or a learned and faithful member of a neighboring church, many congregations would be blessed to have some recurring voice which is related to the congregation only as a brother or sister in Christ.

Good governance requires effort. It is easier to pull a model constitution off of the Internet than to struggle with crafting a new set of documents best suited to your particular context. It would be easier still to just roll dice or cast lots – as occurs numerous times in the Bible. But, the effort invested in designing good systems of congregational governance is well worth the effort.

Whatever your governance structure looks like, your meetings require some kind of order. *Roberts Rules of Order*, though not the only means of ordering a meeting, is the most common means used in churches and most other organizations that hold public meetings. The ubiquity of *Roberts Rules* is ironic, given the dearth of members who are actually proficient in the use of those rules. Organizations that purport to abide by these rules would be well served to provide recurring basic training in the rules of procedure and would use a parliamentarian at each congregational meeting unless the presiding leader is completely confident in their knowledge of *Roberts Rules*. Finally, these rules, like the governing documents that they are inter-connected with, must be applied with grace, consistency and patience.

Are you bold enough to consider changing how your church structures itself for making decisions? If so, consider these steps:
- Dig out all of your congregation's governing documents, rules, and policies. If you find multiple versions, look for a date that the document was approved. (Always include the approved date on all copies of such documents!)
- Compare the documents looking for inconsistencies amongst them.
- Compare the documents looking for inconsistencies between the documents and your actual practices.
- Get a copy of *Roberts Rules of Order*. Read it (not just the summary table of motions).
- Research to see if your governing documents are in compliance with any relevant denominational documents as well as the laws of the jurisdiction in which your church is incorporated.
- Next, start to dream. Ask yourselves: How closely do our documents reflect our sense of the purpose of the church? Can our structure be better designed to support the purposes to which God has called us?

Worship

How blessed are the people who worship you! O Lord, they experience your favor.

Psalm 89:15 (NET)

The Psalms, the original church hymnal, give us a glimpse into Israelite worship. Consider some of the topics that the Psalms, and the remainder of scripture, do not definitively address for us today:
- the proper ratio of music, sermon, and prayer;
- the style, volume, and tempo of the music;
- which instruments to use;
- the length of the sermon;
- the style and content of the sermon;
- the method of praying;
- the dress code for the worship leader;
- the dress code for everyone else;
- the architecture of the meeting space;
- whether to sit on pews or chairs;
- do worshippers respond with "Amen" or other affirmations during the sermon;
- are testimonies to be given;
- what portions of the service children are present during;
- whether the liturgy should follow a rigid format or be spontaneous;
- whether or not to preach from behind a pulpit;
- how long the service should last;
- whether guests should be permitted to attend, and if permitted whether and how they should be identified;
- how often holy communion should be celebrated;
- what to use as bread and wine and how to distribute them;
- how many times per service should an offering be collected;
- whether to use video projection;

- whether music can be played from a recording or must be performed live;
- which bible translations are used;
- whether the flowers on the altar (if any) can be artificial; and
- what are the size, shape, and adornments of the vessel containing water for baptism?

As you review the above list, which of the topics have been a cause for disagreement in your congregation? Which ones seem unimportant to you? Which ones seem to have a single, rigid answer for your congregation? Which ones distinguish your congregation from others in your community? In differing settings, each of the preceding topics have been contentious issues.

Worship is one of the most distinctive features that enable people to distinguish among different churches. The vast diversity of worship styles and practices enable connections to people that are vastly different. The same twenty minute sermon may be considered unbearably long at one church and, at the church across the street received as unconscionably shallow in its brevity. Organ music may be viewed as indispensable at one church and inconceivable at another. Because of this vast diversity, there is little in the way of objective norms for assessing worship in individual settings.

Decades ago, I did my first consulting work at a congregation that was using an assessment tool to help them create a long-range plan. I had worshipped a number of times at the church and the preaching was some of the most uninspiring, uninteresting, and monotone that I had ever heard. Yet, the congregational surveys ranked the preaching as excellent. I re-tabulated the numbers and verified the math. I studied the form to see if there was any chance that people could have inverted the high/low ranking system. Nothing could explain this anomaly. I listened to the preaching again and verified my recollection of how bad it really was. So, I started to talk to the members. I discovered that this pastor was the most loving and pastorally caring leader that the members could remember. They had perceived that honestly answering the question about the quality of their beloved pastor's preaching would cause him pain – so they lied. Often, surveys about preaching quality are a better barometer of the pastor's relationship with the congregation than of anything else. Hence, assessments of preaching tend to decline in times of congregational conflict, even when there are no objectively discernable changes to the style of preaching. (Anger and bitterness expressed through preaching under such stresses are a different matter.) To a lesser degree, assessments of music can be subject to comparable limitations.

People tend to join a church that provides a style of worship that they like. There are a few exceptions to this generalization, like:
- **Geography**: In areas with relatively few church choices, people may not find a close fit to their preferences.
- **Denomination**: Though this variable has declined substantially in impact, some people still feel a sense of denominational loyalty which overrides their worship preferences.
- **Attractant ministry**: For some people, a recovery group, a youth program, a singles' ministry or some other program is so important to a person that they attend the church with that feature, regardless of worship style.
- **Family ties**: Some people are born into or marry into a church and stay for family reasons.

With those exceptions noted, worship is a key determinant that helps many people to find the church that they will call home. If people choose a church home based on some criteria other than worship, it raises the likelihood that the particular worship style may never seem preferable to them. There is also, certainly, a difficult to measure subsection of folks for whom the style of worship just is not particularly important. Most people have a boundaried elasticity in their worship preferences. In other words, they are comfortable across a certain range of styles, but uncomfortable outside of that range. The size of the range varies greatly. Some people are open to almost any service, as long as there is pipe organ accompaniment and a choir. Others may define their boundary at baptism by immersion, communion with grape juice and wafers, or a service that always fits a 60 minute time slot. The choir, hymnody, and message may be perfect, but someone may judge the service as a failure if the total length stretches to 61 minutes!

How then can we assess worship? Try asking yourself these questions:
- Is God honored by what we do?
- Does the service give hope, encouragement, and knowledge to those gathered? (Your tradition may dictate the relative importance of those three elements.)
- Does the mood and mode of worship leadership project a feeling of genuineness and reverent professionalism without feeling slick or impersonal?
- Do members come regularly and do they bring guests?

Doing worship well need not mean perfect execution. Preachers and musicians have off days. As long as the off days are the exception and not the expectation, then they can serve to illustrate that everyone is imperfect and still welcomed into Christian community. The worship experience is shaped by much more than what is sung, played, and preached. The thermostat and sound system, for example, have the potential to ruin even the best prepared service. Think of worship as a total experience.

With all of the sacramental, instrumental, and preaching variations that exist, it might seem illogical that a single point of contention could come to dominate disagreements across a broad diversity of churches. Yet, the debate framed as traditional versus contemporary has risen to that level. In reality, *traditional* and *contemporary* can mean very different things depending upon the specific context. Perhaps a more helpful vocabulary would be: *what we are accustomed to* and *something new*. If we were to limit ourselves to the music available to the psalmists, then no church would use a pipe organ. In certain times and places, pipe organs were the new and contemporary innovation. In the first quarter of the 20th century, organs were commonplace in theaters. In the 1970's it was still not uncommon to find organs used in indoor sporting arenas to energize the crowd in support of the home team.

Pipe organs still produce beautiful music that is appreciated by many. Culturally, they have become less relevant – because fewer people hear them played, especially outside of worship services. But, less relevant does not necessarily mean irrelevant. Nothing is comparable to the organ for people of certain generations, geographies, and experiences.

At the start of the 20th century, people with the requisite financial means were buying wax phonograph cylinders or player piano rolls. Music consumers in the decades that followed greeted these innovations:
- Records (78, 33, and 45 rpm)
- Radio (AM and FM)
- Broadcast Television (Lawrence Welk, American Bandstand, Hee Haw, Variety Shows, etc.)
- Reel-to-Reel audio tape recordings
- Audio Cassettes
- 8 Tracks
- Video Cassettes
- Cable and Satellite Television (MTV, VH1, CMT, various religious channels)
- CD's
- DVD's
- MP3 players with internet downloading

In the closing days of the 20th century, XM and Sirius were preparing to introduce satellite radio and Apple was likewise preparing to release the first generation iPod. In the brief history of a century, people readily adapted to a variety of technologies which had the cumulative effect of producing this powerful reality: people can listen to whatever music they want. No church today is large enough to offer a weekly menu of services catering to every potential musical preference. Nonetheless, churches must think strategically about whom they are likely to welcome and spiritually feed with the musical styles that they choose.

In the 1990's, a modestly growing mid-size church with a long history found itself caught in the tension of this mentality of consumer choice. The church had an early Sunday liturgical service with organ music from the denominational hymnal, a mid morning copy of the early service, and a late morning service in the praise worship genre. The second service was the best attended, followed by the late and with the early morning trailing far behind. Wanting to be good stewards of space and time, they converted the mid-morning service to a blend of the two styles. It grew modestly, but who attended was the most interesting insight: most members of that congregation continued to attend whatever service they had been attending. In the final analysis, schedule convenience mattered more than the music.

A clear trend has emerged among many growing churches. In these strategically adapted churches, a single worship style is neither the glue that holds together, nor the distinctive that sets apart the congregation. These churches provide two or more distinctive worship styles per week. The sermon is often (though not always) the same at each service. The sacramental practices are the same (though communion distribution may be handled differently). The separate services are held together by other ministries, a common theology, shared staff, and a well communicated common vision for the future. Even the building may or may not be shared, as seen in the growing popularity of satellite worship centers.

Whatever your worship service looks, feels, and sounds like, keep the following in mind:
- **Predictability is good**: Regular schedules (without summer exceptions) are best for visitors. Having the same style of service, at the same time, each week, is generally best. Congregations with seasonal membership or seasonal non-resident visitors may necessitate exceptions.
- **Offer options**: Henry Ford's decision to sell Model T's in any color "as long as it is black" probably made sense to him at the time, but a glance at a parking lot today tells a different story. Separate and distinctive worship

styles create more opportunities to share the Good News with more people.
- **Blend smoothies, not worship**: Successfully integrating substantially different styles into a single service is a tall mountain to climb. Doing it every week will test your mountaineering skills! There are reasons why classical organ, Hawaiian electric guitar, and rap are not often found on the same CD or radio station: they just don't go together. With the exception of infrequent special events or very unique contexts, blending dissimilar worship styles is rarely the best choice.

Your homework to learn more about worship is fun. Ask around and find those places where the worship services have a reputation for being interesting, appealing, or inspiring. Find 4 to 6 other leaders and go visit those worship services. Go out immediately afterwards for brunch or coffee to debrief what you experienced. Appoint an informal secretary to jot down your collected comments. Don't let theological disagreement with the sermon, or discomfort with different sacramental practices, prevent you from learning what they are doing well. Don't feel compelled to justify why your church is "better" or focus on excuses for what might be hard to do. Repeat the process at several churches. Prayerfully share what you have learned with your congregation's core leadership. Then, engage the conversation about possibilities for your church.

Small Groups

The Sovereign LORD declares—he who gathers the exiles of Israel: "I will gather still others to them besides those already gathered.

Isaiah 56:8 (NIV)

In 2004, I was invited to travel to Sheffield, England with a small group of church consultants and leaders. We had been assured that there was something worth seeing there, which would justify the expense of time and transatlantic airfare. To tease our interest, it was disclosed that the church we were to visit was half Baptist and half Anglican and the whole thing was growing. Baptists and Anglicans have rather different practices regarding baptism, polity, and other matters – so our attention had been hooked. We arrived and were transported to the host homes of church members who generously lodged us. Later, over dinner in an English pub, Pastor Mike Breen began to tell us the story. By dinner's end we knew that the trip had been worthwhile. As the story unfolded, we came to appreciate that the merged Baptist and Anglican histories were merely an interesting backdrop for the greater insights about structuring for small group ministry.

For years, those of us consulting congregations had known that there was a high correlation between small groups and healthy, growing churches. The intimacy and informality of the small group is a powerful counterpoint to the anonymity and formality of a large worshipping community. Small groups help people to grow spiritually and stay connected to the broader congregation. Dale Galloway, Rick Warren, and others had already been vocal champions of the small group cause. Small groups had been around for long enough that we already knew that there were more healthy and less healthy ways to organize them.

With small groups, as with many other things, some models are so tied to their context, that they defy attempts at replication. Dr. Yonggi Cho's South Korean church involves hundreds of thousands of Christians in houses and cells and, though many have studied the small group model employed there, no one has yet replicated it on a comparable scale in any other context. So, when the folks from Sheffield talked, we were both eager to listen and skeptical that this might be another "one hit wonder" that wouldn't work elsewhere. We learned that the passion about small groups was widespread at St. Thomas's Church in Sheffield. People's eyes lit up when describing the role that small groups had played in transforming their lives. Our eyes lit up when we heard that this unique approach to small groups had already been replicated at churches in several different countries.

Small groups at St. Thomas's are not viewed as an optional program. Rather, they are seen as a fundamental building block of the faith community. It is a handful of people that each trust each other and see one another as temporary but devoted companions on a lifelong journey of faith. The temporary element is critical, because they understand the necessity of regularly dividing the groups so that they can continue to grow. The devotion is equally important as it signifies trust and commitment. If you were hospitalized, you would expect your small group to visit and pray with you. Small groups provide opportunities for leadership development, teaching & learning, and modeling of mutual pastoral care. St. Thomas's utilizes affinity small groups, so the members have some shared interest like:

- being fans of the same soccer team;
- having the same chronic illness; or
- working in the same department.

Another key insight was how this essential building block is stacked with other building blocks in the making of a church. For decades, church growth researchers have indicated that small, mid-size, and large groups all have unique roles in a healthy church. The leaders at St. Thomas's contributed fresh insight about the function of the mid-size groups. Clusters, as they call them in Sheffield, are groupings of small groups. Depending upon the number of small groups and the size of each, this could yield a count of 35 to 50 people. Because affinity small groups are the basic building block, the clusters have a distinctive commonality that the groups hold in common, for example:

- soccer fans, though fans of different teams;
- chronically ill, but with different illnesses; or
- working in the same building, but different departments.

The leaders at St.Thomas's contributed fresh insights about the function of mid-size groups. The affinity element fulfills a powerful glue-like function, which seems more effective than shepherding systems which use geography or alphabet as imposed groupings. More powerful yet, has been the recognition that small, mid-size, and large groups serve different intimacy needs. As human beings, we each have a need for relationships that have differing degrees of trust, expectations of, and knowledge about each other. Group size shapes those three variables. Depending upon our background and present circumstances, we may have most of our needs at certain levels met through work, family, or other connections. At St. Thomas's they use small groups, clusters, and celebrations to respond to those different intimacy levels. They have learned that clusters (the group most lacking at most churches) is the easiest point of entry for a newcomer. Cluster gatherings typically feature a little food, a little music, a little sharing about the joys or challenges of the week, and prayer. Celebrations are what most of us think of as weekly worship services. Actually, they also have an even smaller group than a small group (accountability huddle) and occasional mega-gatherings of multiple celebrations, but I will let you read their book for those details.

You may be tempted to say: *Well, all of that sounds fine, but we tried small groups before and it didn't really work well for us.* I would respond that, done well, small groups are well worth the effort and pay big dividends in spiritual growth. There are, indisputably, many ministry leaders and followers from small group ministries that started well and then drifted into dysfunction.

A small group ministry with maximum effectiveness is attentive to the 6C's :

- **Customary:** Don't let small groups be just another thing on a busy church calendar. Treat them as a fundamental building block and encourage everyone to participate. Make it a criterion for selecting all church leaders.
- **Commonality:** Affinity groups make sense. Help people make connections based on some unique trait, interest, challenge, or desire that they share in common.
- **Covenants:** Each group should have ground rules about confidentiality, commitment to participate for a set period of time, being prepared for group time, and being prepared to split and create new groups.
- **Content:** Over a year, each group should explore a mix of material that is sometimes unique to the group members' interests and sometimes simultaneously shared across the whole church.
- **Coordination:** Somebody should oversee all small groups in the church and be a resource for materials, leader training, and recruitment.
- **Clusters:** Groups of small groups should get together at least monthly for fellowship or service projects – and these gatherings may be the least threatening way to invite new people to your church.

Jesus spent most of his recorded ministry in three levels of groups: a small group (the 12); a mid-size group (those who followed); and a large group (the crowds). The model still works for us today. If you are ready to think more about ministry intentionally structured among different group sizes, I suggest:

- Breen, Mike, and Walt Kallestad. The Passionate Church. Lifeshapes the language of leadership. Colorado Springs, Colo: Cook Communications Ministries, 2005.:

Worldview

I am confident in the Lord that you will take no other view. The one who is throwing you into confusion will pay the penalty, whoever he may be.

Galatians 5:10 (NIV)

Biblical Archeology was a one credit hour seminary class that was taught by a nice professor and fit my schedule conveniently. My enthusiasm for Indiana Jones style adventures was quickly replaced with the reality that most Biblical Archeology deals with pottery shards and, unfortunately, 3000 year old broken pottery didn't look much different to my undiscerning eye than the flower pot I had accidentally dropped on the garage floor a few months before. But, I did learn one amazing bit of information which now helps to shape my understanding of ministry. We heard about archeomagnetism (or paleomagnetism, or detrital remanent magnetism). All of these concepts deal with the fact that the earth's magnetic field changes over time and the degree to which objects are out of alignment with the current magnetic field can be used for dating some archeological discoveries.

The reason that this is archeologically useful is that clay has very tiny bits of iron in it which remain in imperceptible motion to keep aligned with the earth's magnetic field – just like the needle of a compass does. When soft clay is fired so that it hardens, the tiny bits of iron no longer have the ability to move. Archeologists use technology, math and physics to "map" the orientation of kilns and other large clay objects from long ago. Clay pots don't have free will, so they never chose to have a particular pattern of tiny iron bits. Even the potter that made them gave no attention to this matter. But, the physics which God set forth to organize all matter and energy had an unseen effect.

We are each not completely unlike clay pots, though we do have free will. If you doubt the plausibility of the analogy, just check Jeremiah 18. Each of us are filled with attitudes, perceptions, and impressions which are not always visible and which we may not always be fully aware of. We are each shaped by all of the relationships, the events that we experience and the information that we consume throughout our life. All of these influences affect how we view the world. Unlike clay that has been fired in a kiln though, we never permanently solidify our internal compasses. We have the capacity – if we choose – to seek out those influences which align our decisions with whatever compass we place our trust in.

Your worldview is, simply put: how you view the world. How you view the world is the starting point from which you make all decisions. There are many different worldviews. Sometimes we juggle more than one view based on the various roles that we each have, like: parent, child, Christian, patriot. Our dominant worldview is the one that informs and shapes all of the others. A biblical worldview is one that is primarily aligned with the teachings of Holy Scripture. Committed Christians have a dominant biblical worldview – scripture is the "North" on their compasses.

Would it be great to have a church filled solely with people who hold a biblical worldview? Yes and no. Certainly we want everyone to be moving in that direction, but if our congregation is universally mature in faith, then it almost certainly means that we are not incorporating new people into the body – people who need to hear, learn, and experience the Good News. I've worked with church leaders who were at first alarmed that so many of their members had unbiblical worldviews, until I showed them that in their particular congregations most of the people with unbiblical worldviews were relatively new to the church. Churches are designed as vineyards for branches and vines to grow, not as a place to merely collect fully grown vines. Of course, if many long time members lack a biblical worldview, that is a cause for alarm. Longevity in a pew has never been a very useful indicator of anyone's spiritual condition.

If our worldview is shaped by the Bible, then how we view the Bible has a big impact on how we ultimately view the world. Christians of different traditions can have very different ways of reconciling the wedding feast at Cana (where Jesus makes wine out of water) with the admonition against drunkenness in Ephesians 5:18. Churches can thrive and be healthy whether or not they permit the enjoyment of alcohol in moderation. The key determinant for congregational health is that all understand the biblical basis of the congregation's teaching and that they retain the capacity to respect and care for those who interpret scripture differently.

Worldview is, inherently, an internal thing. When I was an officer in the Navy's chaplaincy program, there was a rigid height and weight chart by which we were assessed. Both variables were objective and easily measured. Worldview is not like that. It is easy for any of us to mask our true intentions and sound more biblically motivated than our hearts truly are. Worldview should never be used as a club to beat others with or as a trophy to demonstrate our own superiority. Still, in Christian community there are ways to encourage and gently admonish with love. It is better to help our brothers and sisters to see the true compass, than to blame them for being lost. If leaders don't model good devotional practices, regular worship participation, engagement with scripture, and lifestyles compliant with the guidance of scripture, then it is rather unlikely that those being led will be inspired otherwise.

Spiritual health is not the same as worldview: but they look quite a bit alike. Worldview does function like a compass, but not like an autopilot. We make daily decisions about whether or not to subjugate our lives to the authority of scripture. Sin, our age old rebellion against God's will, enters the equation and we sometimes end up off course regardless of the accuracy of our compass. Thank goodness that grace and forgiveness are also part of a biblical worldview!

Remember, you are not a clay pot – despite sharing a few characteristics with one. Your internal compass remains as responsive to God's tug as you permit it to be. The world exerts more influence on you than you can imagine. Be sure that your daily practices incorporate enough of God's influences to keep your course true.

If you are ready to engage the issue of worldview, I recommend this book by my friend and consulting mentor, Dr. Kent Hunter, who opened my eyes to the power of worldview:

- Hunter, Kent R. <u>Discover Your Windows: Lining Up with God's Vision</u>. Nashville, Tenn: Abingdon Press, 2002.

For recent research, a good starting point is the Barna Group:

- <u>www.barna.org</u>

Facilities

But who is capable of building such a structure? Why, the skies--the entire cosmos!--can't begin to contain him. And me, who am I to think I can build a house adequate for God--burning incense to him is about all I'm good for!

– 2 Chronicles 2:6 (MSG)

I once pastored at a congregation which had, for thirty years, worshipped in what the architect had intended to be a hallway connecting the future worship center to the future fellowship hall. The intention had been to use this narrow room with a low ceiling for weekly worship just until the mortgage was paid off, at which time the worship center would be built using a new mortgage. The congregation got comfortable in the space and then got very comfortable with the idea of being debt free. Decades later, the congregation discerned a need to offer a new worship style, which was acoustically and logistically impractical in the long-term *temporary* worship space. Unfortunately, though not unpredictably, the congregation had declined in numbers over the decades and was quite limited in the size of facility that they could now finance constructing.

They used volunteers and donated materials and were able to eventually construct an impressive new facility. In the midst of construction, however, an anonymous letter arrived in the church office. The shell of the incomplete new building resembled a pole barn and the nameless letter writer unleashed a torrent of vitriol about the "shabby farm building" that was in process. As I read that letter aloud to the office secretary, I was hurt, angry, and frustrated. The wise and faithful secretary quickly put the matter in context asking: *Wasn't Jesus born in a farm building?* Indeed!

Jesus' earthly ministry began in a humble stable. In the early centuries of the Christian church, recognizable buildings were politically unsafe. But that trend changed radically when Emperor Constantine elevated Christianity to the status of preferred religion and started the biggest construction boom in world history. Church buildings today come in all shapes and sizes. Even the word "church" is used interchangeably to refer either to a local congregation of believers or merely to the building in which they gather.

The great cathedrals of Europe are awe inspiring to visit. The massive modern auditoriums of megachurches in the USA continue to redefine what is technologically possible with audio and video reinforcement. The corrugated tin sheds with dirt floors that are common in Africa, are home to some of the fastest growing ministries in the world. And, the little country church with a tall steeple still evokes feelings of comfort in the hearts of many. There is no such thing as a typical church building. Many churches today don't even own a building, opting instead to rent movie theaters or high school gymnasiums.

Three issues, held in tension, summarize the challenge presented by church buildings: function, image, and cost. Generally, the more focus given to any of these three concerns occurs at some detriment to the other two. The functionality of a building describes what activities can be supported and how many people can be accommodated. Image is how the building looks. Image includes architectural style, choice of materials (concrete, marble, glass, wood, etc.) and the number of artistic elements that are incorporated into the overall design. Cost seems self-explanatory, but the long-term maintenance costs of varying materials, the varying resale values of differing architectural styles, and other factors make cost more than a simple question of the amount paid to the builder.

The tension of these three variables can be envisioned in this way:

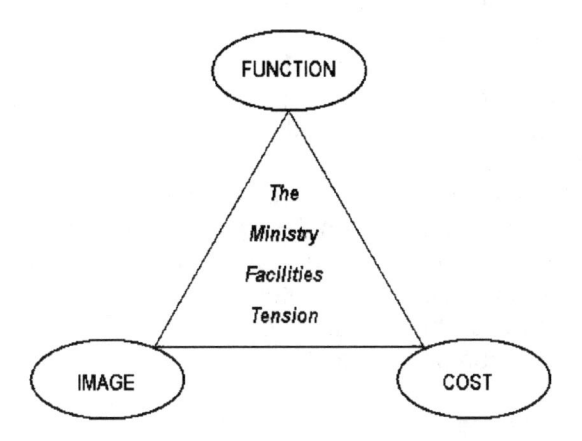

```
           FUNCTION
              /\
             /  \
            / The \
           /Ministry\
          /Facilities\
         / Tension    \
        /_____\
     IMAGE            COST
```

Normally, functionality is why we build, buy, remodel, or retrofit buildings for ministry. Our buildings may provide spaces for worship, fellowship, and education. Additionally, those ministries may be supported through offices, parking, storage, and other functions. Highly functional facilities are those that best support ministry.

Image is the message that the building sends. Some facilities silently scream TRADITIONAL with a tall steeple atop a steep, slate roof. Some facilities raise the banner of MODERN, with lots of metal, glass, and curves. Some facilities suggest INSTITUTIONAL, with tall brick walls and uniform windows. Some facilities whisper the name of a famous architect. Christendom has lots of room for lots of different styles. Many churches do fantastic ministry in simple rectangular structures. Many, though certainly not all, church building committees fall into a common trap that progresses like this:
1. We start with a list of what the building should be able to functionally accommodate.
2. We realize that the committee includes members with different preconceptions about what a new building should look like.

3. We bring in an architect to sketch some initial drawings.
4. We disagree.
5. The architect guides us toward a particular style and image.
6. We find out that we can't afford the building.
7. The architect drafts a new plan based on the agreed style and image, but with the ministry functionality scaled back to fit the budget.
8. We line-up financing and break ground.
9. Five years later, the building is a decade away from being paid for, but the compromised functionality is frustrating ministry and limiting growth.
10. We have to choose: add debt on top of debt or let the congregation plateau and eventually decline.

Christianity has contributed amazing creations to the arts rendered in paint, sculpture, music, and architecture. Most congregations don't commission marble sculptures or bronze castings, yet many succumb to the notion that if we need a building it must make an architectural statement. God certainly uses some churches for such a purpose, but human ego rather than God's vision too often drives the style of our buildings.

Lack of knowledge runs a close second to ego as a stumbling block for church facilities design. A common problem is functional misproportion. If a building design meets our education space needs for the next 20 years, but only accommodates 5 years of worship growth, then it is misproportioned. Of course, it is impossible to know with precision the size of each of your congregation's ministries far into the future. Because of that uncertainty, church designers apply various rules of thumb: X square feet for each person in worship, Y square feet for each child in Sunday School, Z square feet for each person seated at a fellowship event, etc. These multiples are a handy starting point, but they each represent an average within a range. For example: the more legroom and girth accommodation that your seats offer, the fewer total seats that you can fit in a particular space. Your educational space may vary wildly if you shift between age-divided, small group, inter-generational, and rotating station models. Educational spaces also need to be attuned to the reality of varying birthrates which result in sometimes large disparities in class size from grade to grade.

These various multipliers are tenuous enough to start, but the greater peril comes in their relation to each other. In some congregations, 100 people in worship might yield 110 people in Sunday school for a multiplier of 1.1. Another church with the same worship attendance might yield only 20 in Sunday School for a multiple of .2. An average of .65 wouldn't serve either church very well. Your denominational tradition, ministry strengths, and demographic context all need to be considered when proportioning the space in your facility.

Ministry gets very frustrating when a church lacks the means to re-purpose unused space in one area when it is over-capacity in another. Flexibility is key. Curtain walls and partitions may not look elegant, but they greatly boost the usability of limited space. Don't presume that education, worship, and fellowship will always function in the way that they do today. Within budgetary constraints, every church facility should be built to accommodate both growth in numbers and changes in ministry style. Staggering multiple worship services and education hours is one way to squeeze greater utilization out of limited space. If consecutive services are your planned solution for expansion, be sure that you allow enough parking spaces for those already in attendance and those arriving for the next round.

As I sat on the podium at a pastors' conference in Kenya, I was alarmed to glance up and note the condition and arrangement of the roof trusses in the main room which was filled with over 600 church leaders. The roof trusses had clearly been stretched and extended in several phases to span the current room width. I learned later that each time the church had grown beyond capacity, they had simply knocked down a stone sidewall, restacked the wall further out, tacked on the needed length to the roof trusses, and covered the gap with fresh corrugated roof panels. Few of our churches will be that adaptable, but what a great example!

One reason why that Kenyan church couldn't be built in the United States is the existence of local building codes. One hundred years ago, many church buildings were still constructed with heavy use of volunteer labor. Today, it is increasingly difficult to utilize donated labor and materials. Additionally, some communities impose highly restrictive parameters regarding external appearance. If you are still in an area that does not have rigid (or arbitrary) code enforcement, then you have an opportunity to save half or more of your facility cost. If you are in a location where do-it-yourself is an option, you will still require the guidance of a good contractor, prudent judgments about situations where free labor may actually cost more than paid labor, and a commitment to embracing the positive side of the national building codes so that your completed facility will be safe, durable, and insurable.

Occasionally, and detrimentally, the building itself comes to dominate the mission of the congregation. The Neiuwe Kerk is an architecturally important building in The Netherlands. It was designed by Jacob van Campenplein in the 15th century. It is aesthetically impressive. Dutch royalty have been married and inaugurated in the historic space. Important figures from Dutch history are buried in the basement. But do you know what else is in the basement? A bar! Beverage sales from the basement and rented exhibit space on the main floor finance the "mission" of the place. The remaining mission is cultural and historical, but not religious. It long ago ceased to be a church. It exists today as a building only.

The Neiuwe Kerk is an extreme case, but many churches today function in a tension between mission and facility in which it is not always clear which is the dog and which is the tail being wagged. We humans attach sentimental value to the buildings in which our personal history has been lived out. An objective outsider may look and see a leaky roof, ancient wiring, and a space that doesn't function very well. We may look at the same space and remember our wedding, the funeral of our spouse, and the baptisms of our children. Leaders are people with cherished memories, too – but it is imperative for ministry leaders to view facilities objectively and remember that the mission and vision of God's church is larger than any piece of land or amalgam of bricks, glass, steel, and wood.

Ask yourself these church facilities questions:
- Will it still be serving the intended purpose when the debt is retired?
- Do the standard "rule of thumb" formulas fit our likely usage?
- Are we building for tomorrow's needs, today's, or yesterday's?
- Is the architect designing for tomorrow's needs, today's, or yesterday's?
- Are we providing sufficient flexibility?
- Are we prepared for technology changes that will impact our offices, computer networks, and use of audio-visual equipment?
- Are common maintenance tasks volunteer-friendly?
- How will we change the light bulbs? (Visitors notice the pattern of burned out bulbs that accumulate until there are enough to justify the hassle of dragging out scaffolding.)
- Where will the next phase of expansion be attached?
- How expensive and operationally distracting will the next phase of expansion be?
- How visitor friendly is the design?
- Is overflow seating clearly visible, or only accessible through a hidden stairway to a balcony?
- Is there an existing structure in our community that we could creatively adapt to our anticipated needs?
- How restrictive are our local zoning and building codes?

As my good friend Kent Hunter has taught many churches, church buildings should be springboards, not vessels, for congregational ministry and vision. Sometimes, it is better to have a small group meet offsite at the local coffee shop. Sometimes, renting or borrowing space is smarter than building. Sometimes we need fancy architecture and sometimes we don't.

As you wrestle with these decisions, consider these resources:

- Callahan, Kennon L. <u>Building for effective mission a complete guide for congregations on bricks and mortar issues.</u> San Francisco: Jossey-Bass, 1997.

- Bowman, Ray, and Eddy Hall. <u>When Not to Build: An Architect's Unconventional Wisdom for the Growing Church</u>. Grand Rapids, Mich: Baker Books, 2000.

Location

In the holy district you shall measure off a section twenty-five thousand cubits long and ten thousand wide, in which shall be the sanctuary, the most holy place.

– Ezekiel 45:3 (NRSV)

We've all heard the saying that the three most important variables in real estate are: Location, Location, Location. That wisdom is no less true for churches. Location is actually two distinct issues for a congregation:
1. What geographic area describes the group of people that we are most likely to serve, and
2. Where will our buildings be?

Two generations ago, many urban churches answered the first question as *the walking distance from* the answer to the second question. Often, the building location was determined by whatever piece of land might be donated. Today, both questions are substantially more complicated. So let's call these interconnected topics: *Service Area* and *Campus Site*. Realize also that satellite ministry centers and video venues grow in usage each year. These innovations produce the possibility of separate, overlapping, or very large single service areas served by multiple campus sites.

Demography (the study of populations) is a powerful ministry tool. Census data, plus a variety of other sources, help us to identify patterns of:
- Overall population growth and decline;
- Household composition (with or without children, number of adults, number employed, etc.);
- Race, income, age, occupations, level of education;
- Methods of transportation used;
- Length of time at current address;
- Number & type of homes being built;
- Number of churches and denominational affiliation;
- Radio station audience sizes;

- Languages spoken;
- Country of origin;
- And much more.

These patterns help us to match a model of ministry outreach to the environment. New churches or established churches that are seeking to grow need a few points of commonality. Geographic proximity and language have traditionally been two of the default starting points of commonality. The delicate balance is to find enough shared characteristics to give cohesion without resulting in segregation or exclusion. Our next chapter deals with this balance in greater detail. Whatever your points of commonality are, demography will help you define your potential audience.

Your service area is the geographic area in which you are most likely to draw members from. It is impacted by a wide group of variables, some of which will be in tension with each other:

- **People group:** People that like Jazz music; parents with school age children; employees with similar vocations; history with a particular denomination; or whatever combination of shared traits bond your group together.
- **Population Density:** Generally, people in more densely populated areas tend to expect that the things they need will be relatively close. They tend to prefer not to travel longer to get to worship than they travel to get to work, shopping, or a movie theater.
- **Level of Service:** Are some other ministries serving this same people group? If so, then your service area will be impacted by the shapes of their corresponding service areas. Denominational mergers have left more than a few congregations with a neighbor church serving a nearly identical demographic and located a mere block away.
- **Niche Size:** Is our people group concentrated in a particular geographic area? The more spread out your target audience is, the wider your service area will need to be.
- **Media market:** If neighboring areas have their own separate newspapers and radio stations, it reinforces the idea that they are different and complicates straddling that invisible boundary.

- **School District:** Rivalry's, peer groups, and conflicting calendars are all potential complications for ministry across school district boundaries. The more youth-driven your ministry is, the more impact this will have.
- **Physical Boundaries:** Rivers, parks, rail lines, and multi-lane interstate highways can all create either real or perceived impediments to travel.
- **Cultural Boundaries:** Perceptions about race, crime, and economic status, though often false, can create zones within a geographic area that people tend to avoid.

None of the above variables is an absolute. Think of each variable as a separate layer of the same translucent color printed on a clear plastic sheet and stacked on top of a map. (Imagine old-fashioned overhead transparencies.) The darkly shaded areas are those with the most overlap. Those heavily overlapped regions define your service area.

Your campus site is the primary location at which ministry events occur. A relatively young ministry or a ministry with difficulties acquiring land, may use a variety of rented or borrowed locations. As with your service area, some of these variables will be in tension with each other:
- **Drive Time Radius:** Using Microsoft MapPoint or a more sophisticated traffic modeling package, you can create drive time zones which show the areas that can be reached from your campus within a specified number of minutes. Five, ten, and fifteen minutes are good radii to have calculated. The higher the percentage of your service area that you can cover in the shortest possible time, the better.
- **Visibility:** Can your building and signage be seen from a high-traffic road?
- **Access:** Is it easy to find your entrance drive from the nearest high-traffic street regardless of the direction a vehicle is headed? Is it easy to get back to the nearest high-traffic street from the church?
- **Perception:** Do people perceive your campus site as unsafe? As distant, remote, or out of the way?

- **Mailing Address:** If you are in an area with abutting jurisdictions, is there great perceived value in having one or another city as your mailing address?
- **Zoning:** Are there restrictive zoning regulations which could unduly burden your efforts to fully develop your campus site?
- **Building Codes:** If you are in an area with abutting jurisdictions, is there a great difference in the severity or arbitrariness of inspections and code enforcement? (Realize that unless you are prepared to build immediately, this could change.)
- **Tax exemption:** Some states with nonprofit property tax exemption yield wide authority to counties or municipalities to make exemption designations. Is your site near a boundary that divides a church-friendly from a church-unfriendly jurisdiction? And, of course, which side of a State boundary line you are on could determine if you have sales tax exemption.
- **Cost & Availability:** Sometimes there are just no available parcels of land of sufficient size available at a manageable price. The choices then are to choose a site too small, too expensive, or too undesirable based on the above criteria.
- **Opportunity:** Sometimes, a deal becomes available on a property that was on nobody's radar as a first choice. Often, these are parcels of land with a building already present. Churches have turned malls, big box retail stores, factories, meat-cutting houses, and corporate office buildings into amazing centers for ministry in such situations. Be neither afraid of nor seduced by such opportunities. Accomplishing such transformations will require heavy measures of both creativity and diligence to details.

Most churches, naturally, already own a parcel of land and have at least one building on it. How is any of this useful for them? Awareness of service area is important because it helps in planning outreach efforts, special events, and coverage areas for mass mailings.

Awareness of the suitability of your campus location is equally important, though more emotionally risky. What would you do if, after a thorough analysis, you realized that your church is in the wrong location? For the sake of ministry, could you forsake your present mailing address? Generally, these conversations are safer when facilitated by an outside consultant.

A concluding word of caution is important here, and will be amplified in the next chapter. It would be horribly wrong to take objective data and twist it into a justification for segregating ourselves into a familiar comfort zone of people who share our skin color, nation of origin, or income level. Outreach can cut across racial and economic divisions if other elements of commonality are the sources of cohesion. Churches that abandon the inner-city for the suburbs need to be very prayerful and acutely aware of all the motives that may be informing such a decision.

Are you ready to learn more about your context? Start with these steps:
- Visit factfinder.census.gov, www.brainyzip.com, www.city-data.com, and zipskinny.com (or similar sites) to learn about your zip code and neighboring zip codes.
- Create a pin plot map of the people served by your congregation. You can do this the old-fashioned way with pushpins on a map, but it is handier when done with computer software.

Evangelism

How beautiful on the mountains are the feet of those who bring good news of peace and salvation, the news that the God of Israel reigns!

– Isaiah 52:7 (NLT)

It has been widely quoted, with variations, that: "Christianity is always only one generation away from extinction." Certainly there is an element of truth in that assertion. Unfortunately, the phrase has a bias towards a dire future situation. In truth, the spiritual health of the current generation depends upon evangelism. We must each tell the story of the Good News of Jesus Christ in part for future generations, in part for those who have yet to absorb it in this generation, but also in part because we grow spiritually when we share the story with others. Equipping believers for evangelism is part of Jesus' instruction that we "go and make disciples."

My grandfather could start a conversation and find a connection with just about anyone. Some people have that knack. There are websites catering primarily to salespeople, which let you systematically probe for some connection to a person you are preparing to meet: shared hobbies, schools, or geography. Social networking websites have exploded in popularity in recent years – all offering new ways to connect. People value connections.

Tracts, free bibles, websites, podcasts, radio stations, and televised church services all offer people an opportunity to see or hear the story of the Gospel. Some people may find Christ or let Christ find them solely through such means. Most people, however, need personal interactions both to start their new life in Christ and to progress in the following lifelong spiritual journey. Hence, the continued necessity of local churches, regardless of technological innovations, remains. A church, at its simplest, is a set of people that are connected to each other and to Christ. An evangelizing church is one that intentionally creates an environment that encourages and equips outsiders to connect both to Jesus Christ and to other church members.

Imagine three balls: one is perfectly smooth; one is covered with cactus needles; one is covered with Velcro. These are good metaphors for considering the capacity of your church to foster the connections that welcome non-believers into a relationship with Christ. The Velcro ball represents a church optimized for effective evangelism. Things (people) stick to it. The cactus ball scares people away. The smooth ball neither clings nor repels, but by its nature it makes it easy for people to slip away.

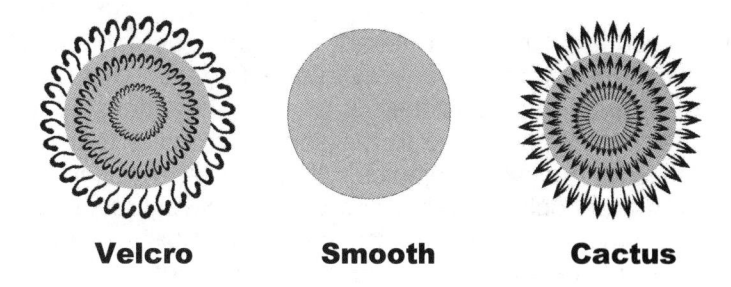

Velcro   **Smooth**   **Cactus**

No church fits purely in either category. Even the most Velcro-like church has a few prickly people and a few slippery areas. And, I have yet to encounter a church, however dysfunctional and conflicted, that didn't still have some people that expressed the love of Christ in a welcoming way. The challenge then, is to be constantly vigilant in creating healthy connection opportunities, while minimizing the prickles and slips.

Some of the differentiation between our metaphorical three balls is obvious. If a visitor is treated with hostility, that is cactus-like. If a visitor is largely ignored, that is slippery. If a visitor is warmly welcomed and shown kindness, that is Velcro-like. None of this seems controversial at all. But imagine that we applied some very different criteria, such as the vocabulary used in the sermon. A bland and simple vocabulary might be understood by all, but fail to engage those with advanced education. An erudite dissertation, sprinkled with references to arcane literary history, might grab the attention of the literati, but turn off everyone else. This is where the controversy of demographic targeting arises.

In reality, churches demographically target all of the time – they simply don't realize it. If your location is not on a public transit route, then you have targeted automobile owners and pedestrians. If you offer services only in English, then English speakers are your target. If you offer no services with sign language interpretation, then you have targeted hearers only. Those who argue that demographic targeting is categorically un-Christian are simply unaware of church history and church practice. Remember, there were regions surrounding the Mediterranean that Paul did not visit. It didn't mean that he was indifferent to the salvation of all those people; it simply means that reaching some of them was not part of his particular calling.

While it is certainly true that smart, strategic, demographic targeting is God-honoring, it is equally true that very un-Christian motives can impact our decisions. It is assuredly offensive to God if we target only people with the same skin color that we have, because of our own prejudice. It is also an error to let divisions exist that could be easily and cost-effectively resolved: simple improvements to the handicapped accessibility of your facility will allow more people to participate without excluding anyone.

Consider light, a common metaphor in scripture, as another analogy. If you expend comparable amounts of energy in a laser, a floodlight, and a spotlight, you get different patterns of light in the same large, darkened room. The laser produces a very intense and very tiny dot of light. The floodlight covers a large area, but with a weak concentration of light. The spotlight gives good illumination, by limiting to the focused area.

Strategically planned demographic targeting uses a mix of all three projection patterns.
- **Laser**: a very narrow target (e.g. an affinity small group for men that restore vintage Ford Mustangs).
- **Floodlight**: a very broad target (e.g. a Christmas Eve service with a blend of music styles and a simple message, starting on December 23rd and repeated at two-hour intervals on December 24th).
- **Spotlight**: a specific target that is big enough to include sub-groups, but small enough to have peer opportunities

(e.g. a worship service including traditional hymnody accompanied by organ, with a 15 minute sermon geared toward middle-class, dual-income households headed by adults with some college completed).

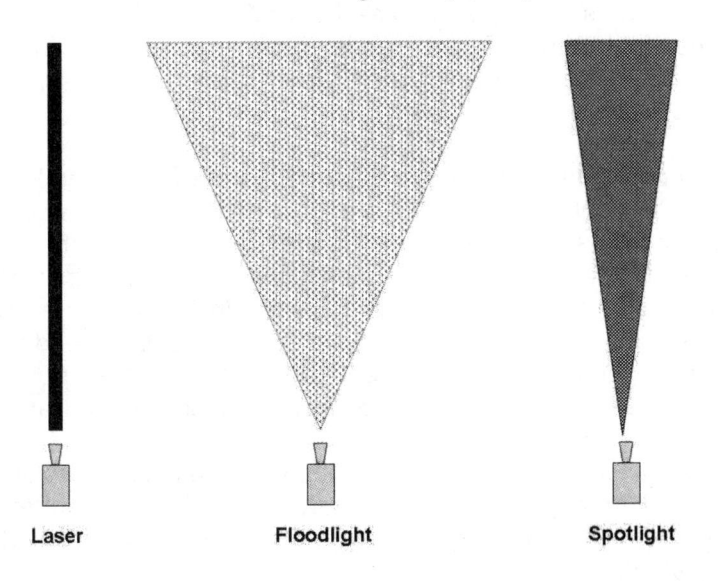

Laser   **Floodlight**   **Spotlight**

A well equipped performance hall typically has more than one of each type of stage lighting. Thriving churches tend to employ a similar strategy: two or more worship services targeting slightly different groups, many small group and niche ministries, and a few mass-appeal events that connect the entire church. Drama productions require that the lighting be well choreographed. Ministry must be planned with comparable attention so that all three lighting styles blend in a manner that pleases God and yields the desired results.

A good starting point for planning is the concept of *felt needs*. Felt needs are those things in life which people have some perception that they are lacking. They sense that something is not right and, though they may or may not have a clear perception of the answer, they realize that they need some solution. Responding to those needs is a genuine response to the Great Commandment that we love our neighbor and it can simultaneously create a powerful opportunity for telling the Gospel story. Felt needs ministries are a classic "two birds with one stone" winning formula. When missionaries first identified this strategy, the felt needs were pretty obvious: clean water, health clinics, schools, and care for orphans. Today, most churches deal with different needs: parenting skills, financial management, addiction recovery, grief support, after-school care, etc.

The felt needs that your church responds to are part of the light that you shine into the world. We should never limit our acts of compassion based on the demographics of our members. However, it makes sense to intentionally overlap our care ministries, our small groups, and our worship formats. Rarely will these opportunities be discerned simultaneously. A need for immigrant legal assistance, may lead to the start of small groups and then to a new worship service in a language unfamiliar to many of your current members. Not all felt needs ministries need to result in new members. All of the various demographics represented in any way at your church should be continually reflected in your planning for laser, floodlight, and spotlight ministry efforts.

Once you have a sense of your target populations, you can start designing programs and special events that fit the needs and interests of your target groups. There are more than enough books and magazines to fill a library with suggestions for such events. Borrow and adapt lots of different ideas to find the best match for your context. Focus on simple events to start. Give yourself permission to fail, as long as you learn from the experience.

Planning to exercise won't build any muscles or burn any calories. Likewise, planning alone won't lead to evangelism. For evangelism plans to yield increase, the plans must be matched with a culture that genuinely values proclaiming the Good News to those who have not experienced it. Members must be passionate about the Gospel, in order for others to perceive this radical message to be real. Churches that ramp-up their evangelism efforts in response to a budget shortfall or the realization of other numeric decline, rarely achieve significant long-term results.

I know a pastor who interviewed once for a position called: Evangelism and Outreach Pastor. During the interview, one of the committee members stopped him and asked "what's this *Great Commission* thing that you keep mentioning?" For at least some in that group, evangelism was purely an institutional necessity – like development work at a university or sales at a business. They were completely unaware of the biblical basis for such work and had no concept of the reality that congregational growth is merely a happy side-effect of evangelism. Evangelism must be driven by the need of the other to hear and our need to tell. Our modern world has taught people to be suspicious. Sometimes others can read our motivations with better clarity than we understand them ourselves. The culture of our churches needs to reflect a selfless motivation for proclaiming the Gospel.

Once a congregation values evangelism for the right reasons and starts to think strategically about how to do outreach, there remain three other components that merit brief mention: the Holy Spirit, free will, and the growing season. The best prepared plans sometimes bear no discernible fruit. Why it is that some hearts are inclined not to embrace the message of salvation is partly a puzzle and partly a matter of theological tension. Why it is that the seed immediately takes root in some and sits apparently idle for decades in others is also often a puzzle and a frustration. It is good to occasionally ponder these things, but futile to allow unanswerable questions to become a stumbling block impeding us from the work of evangelism that each of us is clearly called to.

Christians each have an inherent call to share the Good News, but that doesn't mean that we are all equipped or gifted for evangelism. Some people have a particular gift for evangelism and congregations should seek specific ways to nurture them in the discovery and use of that gift. That still leaves plenty of evangelism work for the rest of us. In the same way that a person without the gift of hospitality can give a cup of water to someone who is thirsty, each of us can be equipped for basic evangelism work. First, every unique spiritual gift can be utilized to support components of a congregational evangelism program. Second, we can each be trained to provide a basic witness of the faith when we find ourselves in an opportune situation.

The U.S. Marines have a mantra of "every Marine a rifleman". The idea is that whether you cook, operate a computer, or fly a helicopter, you should also be thoroughly competent in the use of issued firearms. Wise church leaders apply this same logic (albeit with more peaceful tools). Christians should be encouraged to focus their service in avenues that match their giftedness, but we should each be equipped for at least a couple of basic tasks:

- **Prayer in crisis**: each Christian ought to be reasonably comfortable saying a prayer aloud in a time of crisis. It need not be long or eloquent, but Christians who find themselves with a sick, grieving, or dying person should know how to pray.
- **Telling the salvation story**: each Christian ought to be familiar enough with the salvation story to guide a doubter or unbeliever through the *Roman Road* or some similar series of scripture passages. Marked Bibles make this task easier and are a great gift to leave behind.

Beyond those two simple skills, every member also needs to be reminded of four fundamental tasks:

- **Tell**: your friends, neighbors, and co-workers what you like about your church. (Never complain about your church around the unchurched!)
- **Invite**: your friends, neighbors, and co-workers to your church. An invitation from you means much more than a TV ad or direct mail postcard.
- **Bring**: your friends, neighbors, and co-workers to your church. Provide transportation and be a personal tour guide.
- **Welcome**: anyone that you don't know. It is far, far better to re-introduce yourself to another member than to risk not welcoming a visitor.

Once visitors get to your church it is important to welcome them – in order to build the connections that we started this chapter talking about. Velcro-like churches go out of their way to welcome visitors, but they do so in a manner that lets the visitor keep as much anonymity as each needs to feel comfortable.

To make your visitors feel welcome, never assume anything:
- Don't assume that they know where the restrooms are.
- Don't assume that they know where the nursery is or what the nursery rules are.
- Don't assume that they know how communion is distributed.
- Don't assume that they know all of the church-specific vocabulary that we use.
- Don't assume that they brought a Bible.
- Don't assume that they know all about Christianity and are just "church shopping".

Realize that visitors may have a different perception of what we call *uncomfortably full* and *uncomfortably empty.* A church is uncomfortably full when it seems too crowded to easily find a desirable seat. In many settings, that is about 75% full, but it is very subjective and varies with architecture type, lighting, and seating arrangement. Visitors tend to be especially desirous of aisle seats with easy access to exits – which tend to be popular among members as well. If you have ushers that show you to a seat, it increases the perceived maximum comfortable seating capacity. If you have a balcony that is not overtly obvious, then the empty seats in it are meaningless to a visitor. Conversely, a church can be also be uncomfortably empty. This is even more subjective, but tends to be a particular problem in churches with one service that is significantly less full than the others because of the scheduled time, the style, or some other factor. Regular attendees realize that the room is properly sized to accommodate the other services – but it can seem peculiarly empty to a visitor. Lighting, curtains, and portable screens can help with this perception.

At most churches, the first perception is formed in the parking lot. Having ample parking spaces reserved for visitors is a great way to greet them. Having greeters in the parking lot and at the entrances is a fantastic way to keep building on that good first impression.

As a church, you will also need three additional strategies as components of your evangelism effort. First, you need a strategy for reinforcing the inviting work of your members. Special events are an easy way for members to invite someone to connect for the first time. Also, though personal inviting and bringing is overwhelmingly the most effective outreach tool, targeting mailings, coordinated use of free media, your website, and other tools all help to build a positive impression coinciding with the personal contacts. You will also need a follow-up strategy, so that worship or special event visitors can be invited back and given more information. And, you need a strategy for assimilation, which includes a path to membership and a process for continued special attention in the early months of membership.

Are you eager to share the Good News? Start with these steps:
- Study the Great Commission, Matthew 28:16-20.
- Visit a neighboring church with a good reputation for parking-to-pew greeters. Discuss your experience.
- Talk to neighboring churches about needs that they have perceived, but haven't been able to effectively respond to.
- Subscribe to *Outreach* magazine and look for ideas that would adapt well for your context.

Vision

Then the LORD answered me and said: Write the vision; make it plain on tablets, so that a runner may read it.

– Habakkuk 2:2 (NRSV)

There was a time when a church merely needed to be the only congregation of a particular denomination or tradition in a given area. Children were born, grew up, and often stayed loyal to the denominational brand. Churches grew simply by natural biological increase with each successive generation.

Those days are barely even a memory for many church leaders today. Large denominations have rules allowing clergy to be shared amongst their rosters. Presbyterian, Baptist, and Pentecostal churches can be found all using the same Vacation Bible School curricula purchased from the same 3rd party parachurch publishing house.

Many churches, for the first time in their histories, need a reason for continuing to exist. History explains why they exist now, something else has to explain their purpose for existing next year, next decade, or next century. That something is vision.

Though the imperative of vision may be newly felt in a large number of churches today, the idea of vision as a powerful force in ministry is scarcely new. The Old Testament account of Nehemiah provides an instructive example. Midway through rebuilding the wall around Jerusalem, Nehemiah encountered a motivational problem with his work crew. Fatigue and fear were eroding their resolve and commitment. Nehemiah refocused their labor by reminding them why their effort was critically important. At the same time, he also adapted the plan in a way that preserved the primary goal but dealt with evolving challenges. Also, he assured the crowd that God would support their effort.

Vision is a powerful encapsulation of where we are going, how we plan to get there, and why we are on the journey. Vision needs reiterated often and in different ways. A catchy and concise statement of the vision is a handy tool for repetition and continuity, but avoid the trap of too many churches who have spent more effort agreeing to the language than they have spent implementing it!

Visioning consists of three tasks which attentive leaders engage continuously and simultaneously:
- **Casting**: When bronze is cast, the craftsman creates a mold and then pours in the molten metal. The craftsman has to first visualize the final product in some other medium and then create a mold that will hold and support the material as it solidifies. We cast vision in a similar way. With organizations, casting is communicating what the outcome will look like and what the boundaries are that support the effort to get from here to there.
- **Assessing**: Are we making progress in the journey to our goal? Do church members understand the vision? Have any of the underlying assumptions that are critical to the vision changed?
- **Discerning**: Prayer, contemplation, brainstorming, respectful and engaged discussion, and more prayer are essential elements of discernment. Leaders focus their knowledge and imagination with God's inspiration and wisdom into a blueprint for the future with sufficient clarity that it will properly hold and support the resources poured into the effort.

If you have already studied the 8D leadership process, then you will recognize that these concepts align with Deduce, Discern, Decide, Disseminate, and Debrief. Vision work is simply one subset of the responsibilities of leadership. It integrates well with the other tasks.

As you read the Casting, Assessing, Discerning list, you may have thought that it was out of order. The listed order would not match the experience of many organizations which have "done" the "vision thing" once, condensed it to a statement, and settled into a pattern of institutional routine. A healthy vision process is, to restate, continuous and simultaneous. There may be important seasons of focus on vision work, especially as milepost goals are met or missed, but for key leaders of the church each component of visioning work should always be active.

Visioning is largely abstract. It is a rich description of a future reality that does not yet exist. Getting members to see that abstract future reality is one challenge. Getting them to agree with it is another. "Buy-in" is another name for the second challenge. Getting them to remain committed to it in tough (or distractingly happy) times is a third challenge.

In my executive coaching with ministry leaders, a common challenge that I see is the necessity and danger of multi-layer abstraction. Imagine describing a possible Facebook-based ministry with Generation Y adults to a group of octogenarians who have never used the Internet. You first need to explain the Internet, then Facebook, then the attitudes and interests of people who grew up in the 1980's and 1990's – all before they could begin to grasp the ministry that you propose to initiate. Ministry can not be limited to one dimensional change, but when we compound the number of elements that people need to imagine, accomplishing buy-in is increasingly difficult. Complicated visions require creative, multi-faceted, and repetitive communications strategies. If people can't understand it, they won't support it.

Vision is a target for your church's shared future. Imagine an archery range with no targets, just people walking around with bows and arrows looking for anything to shoot at. If ministry leaders fail to clearly cast a compelling vision, then people will presume their own individual visions for the church's future. Many of those presumed visions will be in conflict. The results of such "vision collisions" can be painful for individuals and devastating for ministries.

Vision is sufficiently appreciated that numerous authors have cast a vision about how to cast a vision! As you search for a style and process that fits your setting, consider reading the following:

- Nehemiah, especially chapter 4.
- Warren, Rick. <u>The Purpose Driven Church: Growth Without Compromising Your Message & Mission.</u> Grand Rapids, MI: Zondervan, 1995. [*Editors note: a new edition of this classic is expected to be published in 2010.*]
- Barna, George. <u>The Power of Vision: Discover and Apply God's Plan for Your Life and Ministry</u>. Ventura, Calif: Regal, 2009.

Technology

God will use them in his work of rebuilding, use them as foundations and pillars, Use them as tools and instruments, use them to oversee his work.

- Zechariah 10:4 (MSG)

Walk through the aisles of your favorite office supply superstore. One of those aisles will be full of pre-printed papers ready for you to copy or print your custom content upon: letterhead, certificates, framed pages for announcements, business cards, etc. Cheap color laser printers have taken a toll on these product lines, but they are still widely present. Have you ever wondered where this handy diversity of print enhancements originated? The answer is church publishing houses. Bulletin covers were the original mass-market, pre-printed, customizable specialty papers. Back in the days of blue, hand-cranked, mimeograph copies, those stock covers gave an elegant appearance – long before the business world appropriated the idea.

Because "telling the story" is such an important part of the ministry of the church, communications technology has been intertwined with the work of the church in every era. Paul's travels (as well as the transport of his letters) were greatly aided by the transportation network of the Roman Empire. Luther's work was widely disseminated with the aid of Guttenberg's printing press. Billy Graham utilized greatly improved large venue sound amplification and the then new media we call television. Ministries today are globally interconnected through the internet. Whether it is flannelgraph or PowerPoint, whatever helps us to convey the message of the Good News is a ministry tool.

If you would have visited a typical church in the USA in 1960, you would have found a 16mm projector, an overhead projector, a record player, and either a 35mm filmstrip projector and a separate slide projector or a combo unit to achieve both those functions. If you were to have visited a neighboring High School, University, or corporate training department, you would have found the same equipment. Jump forward 20 years and you would have found that the High School, University, and corporate training department had mostly transitioned to videotape. The typical church didn't get a VCR, however, until it had become a commonplace item in member's homes. Over two decades, the typical church went from being on par with the other professional communicators in the community, to lagging behind the consumer market.

Comparative Use of Communications Technology

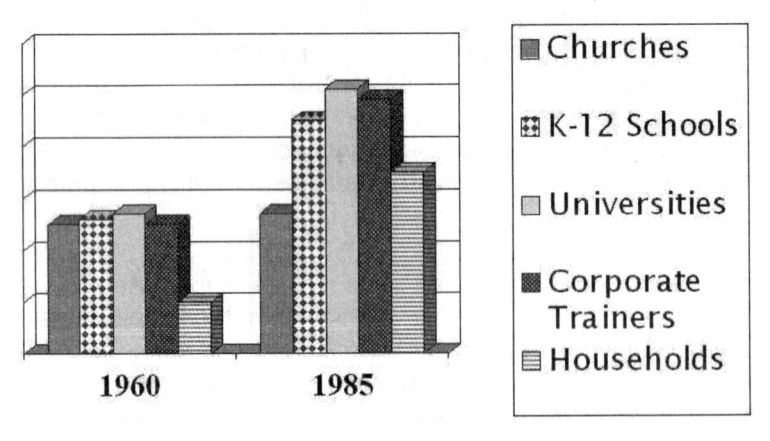

- Churches
- K-12 Schools
- Universities
- Corporate Trainers
- Households

(1960, 1985)

Not every church succumbed to this communications retreat. During those same years many churches embraced the new audio cassette format and developed tape ministries of various types – generally mirroring the missional mindset and goals of the congregation. Some used the tapes strictly to serve their shut-in and hospitalized members. Others used them as an evangelistic tool. Also, during those same decades, most congregations transitioned from a mimeograph machine to a photocopier (and some later transitioned back using newer and better duplicating technology). The problem was not that churches sat still; the problem was that most churches adapted to the range of evolving technology tools at a pace far slower than other organizations and households in our culture.

From the wide array of emerging tools, churches tended to pick upgrades that were utilitarian. Computers were purchased, often driven by the reality that they could more efficiently track contributions and generate mailing labels. Copiers were handier than mimeographs and stencil-cutters. More durable Solid State PA systems replaced those that relied upon fragile tubes.

In the decades that followed, the track record of churches grew more spotty. Did your school or business have a website before your church? Who has the better maintained website today? How does the size of television in your living room compare to the sizes at your church – considering how many people are intended to simultaneously view it and from what distance? Does the church office have a slower internet connection than the members do in their homes and workplaces?

There have been problems with this non-strategic embrace of technology. First, it degraded the perceived relevance and importance of the message that we were communicating. Second, it actually resulted in technology downgrading at many churches. Third, it affirmed a decision-making model of necessity over opportunity.

Perception is important in communications. What we intend that people will interpret us to have said is not nearly as important as what they actually perceive us to have said. Generations weaned on television respond differently to a speaker in a pulpit talking for 20 minutes without a commercial break or change of camera angle, than do generations raised without that influence. The internet, cellphones, and text messaging are only accelerating that trend. So, the pace of communications change can reduce the effectiveness of our proclamation. But, it can also give the impression that our message is less important than the blizzard of messages pelting people in our society. What subtle messages about priority and importance are inferred if you can check the schedule and register for Little League online, but not for Vacation Bible School?

Around the time of the most recent turning millennium, small to mid-size church offices began to encounter a new phenomenon of brides requesting to do their own wedding bulletins – because they knew what desktop publishing software could do and they knew that they could produce a much nicer bulletin than what they were accustomed to receiving at church. The church bulletin had come full circle – from being an innovative concept copied by other trades, to the subject of comparative derision outperformed by the copies it spawned.

Tragically, churches aren't just failing to keep up with the constantly moving target of technology standards. In the 1960's and 1970's, it was common to see those 16mm and 35mm projectors in use. A typical church had a Sunday School supply room in which resided media drawers full of filmstrips. Lending services offered a wide array of movie titles for rental. Judicatory offices produced stewardship appeals and mission updates using those media. Publishing houses cranked out educational and inspirational titles in the same formats. If you were active in a church before 1975, assuredly you remember their use.

But a curious thing happened. Church folk learned, albeit unintentionally, the concept of scalability. A 35mm projector could be used in a small classroom or a large sanctuary. The further that the projector was moved from the screen, the bigger the picture. A really big room required darkening, but the same equipment and media were used. But such was not the case with the consumer-market video that most churches eventually adopted. A VCR and 25 inch TV are great for a small classroom, but they are of little value for a large audience. Still, churches that opted not to adopt video projection were cognizant that the world had changed. A static film slide show doesn't compare well with a dynamic PowerPoint presentation. The 16mm and 35mm media market faded into history. So, those churches regressed back to the "state of the art" of the early 1900's for large audience settings – a speaker with a microphone and nothing more. The marketplace didn't offer an option for sitting still; the choices were move forward or move backward.

The 1908 Sears Roebuck catalog has a large, eye-catching listing with the banner headline:

HOW THIS CHURCH DOUBLED ITS ATTENDANCE
Through the use of our "Holy Land"
colored stereoscopic views

The potential for technology to boost attendance has been recognized for over a century. It has also been oversold. LCD panels are not magic beans that will grow a beanstalk to the home of the church attendance giant. A bad sermon with supporting PowerPoint images is still a bad sermon. An uninspiring vision for the future is still uninspiring when printed with CMYK color separation. A calendar of events that is irrelevant to the felt needs of your target demographic groups is still irrelevant when displayed on an attractive and intuitive website. Off key vocals will still be off key when sent to the speakers from a cutting-edge digital mixing board.

I once had a professor that was an amateur wine-maker. He had a batch of wine that had a funny and not especially desirable taste. So, he used it to make brandy. (Brandy is made from wine that is distilled to create a more intense flavor.) You can guess the result: he got brandy which had an even more concentrated funny and not especially desirable taste. Technology concentrates the effect of our ministry – for better or worse.

What we call *technology* is simply a wide assortment of tools and instruments. Tools don't create buildings: people use tools to change and assemble materials to create buildings. A harp doesn't make music, rather, a harpist uses a harp to make music. For ministry, these tools and instruments primarily fall in two broad and not completely distinct categories:

- <u>Logistics</u>: Church Management Software, accounting software, spreadsheets, programmable thermostats, electronic access control, etc.

- <u>Communications</u>: sound systems, video projection, video editing, presentation software, podcasting, websites, CD/DVD duplicators, digital signage, document production, e-mail, etc.

While it remains true that the bad sermon remains bad with the addition of PowerPoint slides, there are tools that can make sermons incrementally better. Web resources can be great assets for sermon preparation. Some preachers are easier to follow with a projected or printed outline. Video recording can be a great asset for self-critique and refinement. In comparable ways, technology can give us incrementally better budgeting, stewardship campaigns, visitor follow-up, gifts discernment, and facilities utilization. Using our evangelism metaphor, technology will not transform a prickly "cactus" church into a sticky "Velcro" church, but it will help a "Velcro" church become stickier by enhancing its effectiveness.

Technology is a significant source of leverage. A great sermon or teaching can be redelivered innumerable times on iPods and YouTube. A well designed flyer can be distributed as a PDF file so that members can print as many copies as they need for friends, neighbors, and coworkers. Sound and video reinforcement allow people in overflow seating areas to see and hear worship, funerals, or special events.

The cost of some technology yields a temptation to embrace a "Haves" and "Have-nots" mentality. It is true that some large churches spend more for a single camera than many small churches spend for their whole annual budget. It is dangerous to allow such facts to foster an attitude of "we would if we could, but we can't." Computers, video projectors, web hosting, software, and laser printers all continue to be replaced with successive models that are better and cheaper. Modest budgets require more creativity, but they leave many options to enhance ministry.

Each church is a different context, so there is no master list of technology acquisitions that every church should make. You should invest in technology that best equips your church to respond to the opportunities and challenges that move your congregation closer to its vision. There are some basic elements that you should think about:

- <u>An Internet Strategy</u>: How will we provide good access for the church office and staff? How will we design, host, and maintain a website? How will we use e-mail to send and receive communications with members and potential visitors?

- <u>An Office Strategy</u>: How will we maintain organizational records and relevant information about members and visitors? How will we design, duplicate, and archive printed materials with an appropriate level of quality?

- <u>A Video Strategy</u>: How will we capture and store still and motion imagery of our people and activities? How will we display videos and images for small, medium, and large groups? How will we be sure that those who preach and teach at our church have at least as wide a range of capabilities as pastors in the 1960's?

- <u>A Sound Strategy</u>: How will we provide sound amplification and mixing for worship spaces and other large gathering areas? How will we accommodate sources like: CD, DVD, iPod, and computer-based presentations?

The recent decades, which have brought so many technological innovations, have come to carry labels like *Information Age* or *Digital Age*. Television, a uni-directional medium, had an immense impact on culture. How much more so will we be impacted by the bi-directional and relational nature of the Internet. Ministry use of such tools is just in its infancy. The Information Age is also radically less cost discriminatory. Relatively few churches could afford TV stations or TV airtime. Now, we all have the opportunity for nearly free worldwide distribution of text, sound, and video. Culture and ministry will be changed in ways that we can only begin to imagine.

One attribute of the Information Age is the power of information. There is great value in the ability to collect data, sift through it, and discern relevant patterns. This will affect churches as well.

By analyzing patterns of giving and attendance, we can be forewarned that a member may be slipping away. Demographic data tells us far more about our ministry context than it was previously possible to know. Assessment tools, like the *Glass Cockpit*, give us unprecedented insight into the health of our congregations.

If someone offered you a hammer, would you stubbornly insist to continue using a rock to pound in a nail? We live in an era when some church leaders have that attitude. What they forget is that 50 years ago churches were using hammers! In 1950, in 1520, and in the first years after our Savior's resurrection, faithful Christians used whatever tools God made available to them for spreading the Good News. The tools change, but the message is constant.

You may want to stick a Post-It note in this page – and be reminded of that invention which sprang from the desire of a church choir member to have a sticky bookmark. Ask yourself a few questions:

- Are we using all of the tools that God has made available for accomplishing God's mission?
- Does our church have strategies in place for:
    - Internet?
    - Office?
    - Sound?
    - Video?
- Have you visited www.churchtech.com?

Symbiosis

And we know that God causes everything to work together for the good of those who love God and are called according to his purpose for them.

– Romans 8:28 (NLT)

One of the most consequential discoveries affecting world history, for harm and for good, was the combination of charcoal, sulfur, saltpeter, and a spark or flame. The three materials were long known and employed for various uses. Combined in proper proportion, they make gunpowder. Looking at the characteristics of the components individually, there is no hint of how powerfully explosive the concoction would be.

An effective church is far more than the sum of its parts. The eleven areas of ministry that we have explored each impact each other. Opposing football teams, colliding ships, and bumper-cars all impact each other as well. Impact is not necessarily positive. In effective ministries the various parts "work together for the good." "Working together" may sound like an overused workplace slogan from the 1980's, but it is as old as God's design seen in the creation all around us.

Nature offers a variety of examples of cooperation known as symbiosis. Symbiosis is a cooperative and mutually beneficial relationship. Lamprey eels clean sharks, which provides food for the eel and hygiene for the shark. Zebras and ostriches are often found together in the savannas of Africa. The poor eyesight of one and the poor sense of smell of the other leave each vulnerable to prey. But when ostriches and zebras feed in the same area, they can be alert to either the sight or the smell of approaching predators. They match their God-given gifts and needs in a way that benefits everyone (except the hungry lion).

Ministries are more effective when ministry leaders view their church as a system composed of smaller sub-systems. There are a myriad of books and resources available about systems theory, but the key concepts are fairly simple. Your church is a large system with a variety of components which vary in the extent to which they are interdependent with other components. Your property committee may have a particular set of members and a unique set of rules and procedures which are quite different from your team that leads Sunday School. But, your Sunday School depends upon the property committee to change the light bulbs. Likewise, the property committee would probably like the cooperation of Sunday School teachers to avoid serving red fruit punch to toddlers in rooms with beige carpet. Neither group functions completely separate from the other.

Synergy is another trendy term that describes the kind of cooperation that ministries need. Synergy is not the same as amalgamation – merely adding more programs doesn't make the whole system better. New programs must be added with awareness of how they will impact other efforts. Synergy is also not parasitic. Ministries should not drain resources from each other without mutual consent and understanding of how the whole church is affected. One commonly used example of symbiosis in nature has been the oxpecker bird and the hippo. It was long presumed to be mutually beneficial because the bird found food through grooming the hippo, but some scientists now question if the oxpeckers "help" might actually make the hippo more prone to parasites and infection. Just because there appears to be mutual benefit, we can't assume that there actually is.

Synergy is dynamic. As long as the underlying ministries or programs are evolving and changing, so too is their relationship. A lunch feeding program for the homeless and an after-school activity program may have a great symbiotic sharing of the church kitchen and fellowship hall with ample time to transition from one activity to the next – until the bus schedule for either group is changed. Suddenly, a great source of cooperation can become a significant conflict.

When I consult churches, one of the areas of symbiosis that I look for is what I call the *cradle-to-car-keys-continuum*. Children in the nursery have far different needs than do 18 year-olds. But, many children follow a rather predictable path through various programs and activities of the church as they grow and mature. Even if these various programs are staffed and administered separately, their leaders need to be in communication so that children are not lost in transitions and so that there is some sense of logic and coordination as to what is taught. Because each church is different, there is no universal template for a *cradle-to-car-keys-continuum*. Each church needs to map out and maintain those relationships and plans in the way that best fits the context and vision.

Managing symbiosis well in a congregation is a critical undertaking. It is a hard concept to teach and the depth required is certainly beyond the parameters of this book. Looking at symbiosis requires acute analytic skills coupled with objectivity – the more accustomed that you are with your church's programs, the less likely you are to be able to summon that objectivity. A capable outsider with specialized ministry knowledge is usually the best choice to facilitate a thorough review for your congregation.

There are five broad schools of thought in the church consulting world which beget corresponding strategies for planning and implementing change in congregations. They are not mutually exclusive, but they do offer a good framework for considering how you want to build toward God's vision for your congregation's future:

- **Never change:** This is the most common model in plateaued and declining churches. A solid, albeit slightly mind-bending, argument can be made that the most radically changed Christian denomination over the last 125 years is Amish! In the late 1800's, the lifestyle of the Amish was only slightly different from that of their rural neighbors. Today, Amish stand out as radically different from the rest of society. In their decision to rigidly eschew change, they have dramatically changed their relationship to the entire culture surrounding them. Avoiding change is meaningless unless we possess the ability to stop the rest of the world from changing.
- **Topical Anesthetic:** This is the second most common paradigm for church planning. It has often been the default response for denominational officials (though this

is changing) and others who have found themselves working with congregations by necessity of role, but without training or assessment expertise. The source of pain is identified and removed. If talking about offering an additional worship style gets some people upset and vocal, then you stop talking about that topic. If people are angry at the pastor, then you get rid of the pastor. Often, this merely defers the underlying issues to another day without giving them honest attention. The medical phrase is: *treating the symptom rather than the disease.*

- **Build on Strengths:** This view is based on sound reasoning and assessment. It was widely popularized with Kennon Callahan's *12 Keys.* In fairness to Callahan, it is an oversimplification of his significant work which moved the field of church assessment forward. It sometimes works. The problem is, for some congregations there simply is not a critical mass of strengths on which to build.
- **Build on Weaknesses:** This view is also based on sound reasoning and assessment. It was widely popularized with Christian Schwartz's Natural Church Development (NCD.) NCD uses the metaphor of staves which comprise the sides of a barrel – the shortest stave represents the weakest area of ministry and the rationale is that a barrel can't hold water above the level of the shortest stave. In fairness to NCD practitioners, NCD also is more complicated than the catch phrases it is reduced to. NCD has been a blessing to many churches by exposing them for the first time to solid, research-based assessment. The key problem is that it leaves out location and other critical elements of local context.
- **Symbiosis:** The ministry symbiosis view starts with these assumptions:
    - that every church is unique;
    - that every church is a system composed of systems;
    - that assessment can bring insights about each specific church, drawing from the patterns observed in many different churches;
    - that proper planning for any church is based upon what will add the greatest strategic strength to the

congregation, consistent with the discerned mission, vision and values; and
- that some objective weaknesses may not be substantial strategic hindrances and that some objective strengths may not offer a platform to build upon.

Imagine that you are given a gift certificate for new tools, in the hope that you will reduce your backlog of overdue home repair projects. In your current toolbox, you have a beautiful torque wrench that is the envy of your neighbors. You have a scratched and rusty pair of needle-nose pliers that you rarely use. You have a floral pink screwdriver that works well, but you are slightly embarrassed to be seen using it. Your greatest tool frustration is that you can never find a ½ inch socket when you need one – and you need one pretty frequently.

The *never change* solution would be to put the gift card in a drawer and forget about it. The *topical anesthetic* solution would be to throw out the pink screwdriver and get an identical, except black-handled, replacement. The *build on strengths* solution would be to buy another torque wrench. The *build on weaknesses* solution would be to find another rusty pair of needle-nose pliers. The *symbiotic* solution would be to get the ½ inch socket that you need (and maybe wrap some electrical tape around the floral pink screwdriver).

The bias of this author and consultant is that symbiosis is the best paradigm for encouraging church health and growth.

Programs

So the Twelve called a meeting of all the believers. "We apostles should spend our time preaching and teaching the word of God, not administering a food program," they said.

– Acts 6:2 (NLT)

Apparently, feeding people was the first church program. Many Bible translations don't use the word at all. The verse above contains the only appearance of "program" in the NLT. "Program" is a word, like "church" that gets confusingly thrown around in a variety of ministry contexts. Consider this sampling:

- It is sometimes used to describe a size of church (larger than the Pastoral size and smaller than the Corporate size).
- It is sometimes used to describe the brainwashing carried out by cults; hence refugees from cults go through *de*-programming.
- It is sometimes used to describe the less desired opposite of a paradigm of ministry focused on equipping laity to serve, leading some to assert: "we are an equipping church, not a program church."
- It is sometimes used instead of "bulletin" to describe the printed outline of the worship service.
- It is sometimes used to differentiate categories of church staff. Typically, the program staff members are those that deal with music, youth, care ministries, and education. Often, secretarial, custodial staff, and nursery staff are considered non-program staff.
- It is sometimes used to describe a special event, like the Children's Christmas Program.

Most often, "program" is loosely used to refer to all of the ministry "stuff" that churches do. All activities of the church should be clearly understood for the way in which they contribute to the overall vision. A common set of values and attitudes should be shared. All staff and volunteers should understand how their efforts contribute to the overall effort.

Churches exist as people in relationship, as people in worship, and as people engaged with the felt needs of the local community and the world. All three expressions are essential, but the last category is the most acutely contextual. Programs are generally focused on that category. The programs that you offer need to match your context, your resources, and your vision.

All programs should be subject to regular review. None should be allowed to function as fiefdoms apart from the rest of the organizational structure. They may need to function and staff in different ways. Some may be short-lived and others nearly perpetual. Your church does not need to match the programs of neighboring churches out of a sense of competition. Churches can be over-programmed or under-programmed.

The twelve Apostles may have been the first ministry leaders to be frustrated with running programs, but they certainly were not the last. Read the rest of the story in Acts 6 and 7. Each church needs the right mix of programs, led by the right people, in a system that works well, and with a common sense of mission, vision, and values.

Leverage

There was plenty of material for all the work to be done. Enough and more than enough.

– Exodus 36:7 (MSG)

The ancient Greeks identified the idea of the lever as a simple machine. The lever (such as a board) is placed over a fulcrum (such as a rock) with the short side under the load to be lifted and the long side used to apply force.

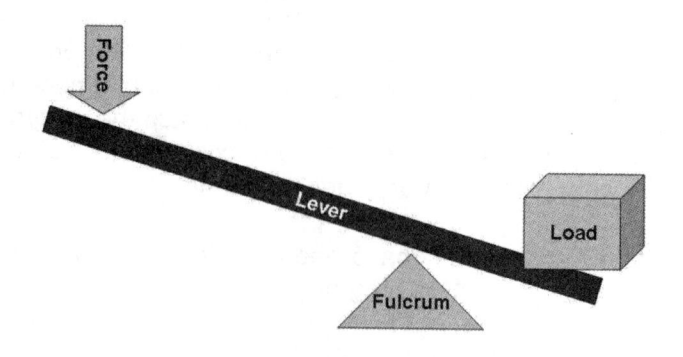

A Working Lever

The lever, like the pulley, is a way of multiplying the effect of our effort so that more work can be accomplished. There are physics formulas which define this multiplying effect, but for our purposes we simply understand leverage as the ability to accomplish more using the limited resources available.

There is no record of Jesus lecturing about Physics, but he clearly cared about the concept of using what resources are entrusted to us for maximum ministry effect. Consider the parable of the talents, found in Matthew 25:14-30. In this parable, Jesus teaches about his expectations when resources are entrusted to each person.

When I was a young child, I thought that "stewardship" meant "potluck." Permit me to explain why. For several years during my childhood, my home congregation hosted annual stewardship dinners. Everyone brought food to share at the potluck dinner, followed by a brief program and the distribution of stewardship materials for the coming year. So as a seven year-old, I was happy to go to a stewardship dinner, because my church had some great cooks! It was a few years later before I learned what stewardship meant. In the church, we often use "stewardship" to refer to the process of soliciting tithes and donations for the current or upcoming budget. That is appropriate because we each are being called to make faithful choices as stewards of our household resources in order that an appropriate tithe would be set aside for the Lord's work through the church. Stewardship also includes our collective administration of those tithes that have been brought together.

Churches have two key stewardship roles: inspirational and managerial. First, we educate, encourage, and inspire people to honor the Biblical tithe in their households. This is primarily important because it helps fosters spiritually healthy households. A beneficial byproduct is the funding for ministry. Second, we strive to manage those resources well, honoring Jesus teaching in the parable of the talents. Financial resources are a point of leverage. Getting the maximum effect from ministry expenditures honors God and assures households that they have rightly chosen to invest their tithes in our church's mission.

Multiplication is another point of leverage. Throughout Jesus' earthly ministry, he invested time and teaching with the twelve. After the Ascension, the twelve invested time and teaching in others. Christianity has grown through multiplication. As the Church became more institutional, however, it drifted into a pattern of consumers and providers. Many Christians became content with the notion that they could simply be consumers for their entire lives. There are many long established congregations today that have not raised up, for more than a generation, a single individual to engage in vocational ministry service. Assuredly, there are many different ways that we can each serve through a wide variety of vocations, but still we are compelled to contemplate the Parable of the Sower in Mark 4 (particularly verse 8). Are most consumer/provider churches generating thirty-fold, sixty-fold, or one hundred-fold increase? They are not.

Multiplication relies upon some model of discipleship. In the corporate world, having an indispensable skill or possessing unique knowledge is a source of job security. But that same model is anathema to scriptural models for the church. We are called to be constantly giving away knowledge as we teach and train others so that they can master a skill set and give it away to yet more believers. If anyone in your church has the only recipe for the coffee cake, or the only experience to teach 7th grade, or is the only one that knows how to set-up the Christmas Tree, then you need to drop everything and start learning together about biblical multiplication!

Symbiosis is another point of leverage. Is there a piece of equipment, a part of the building, a trained volunteer, or a planned event that could be better utilized if different ministries collaborated together? Do you have a bus that only the youth use? Perhaps other ministries could use it as well. Symbiosis need not stop at the edge of your church property. Perhaps neighboring churches could share a specialized staff person, or do a joint event, or share a piece of infrequently used equipment.

Ministry staffing tends to be expensive when considered as a proportion of total expenditures, but cheap when compared to salaries for comparable skills and education in other fields. This cost dichotomy is a source of frustration in many churches. Church members sometimes resent the high cost of a pastor's salary as a percentage of the church budget – especially if they only perceive the work that he or she does for an hour a week. Pastors know that their skills, years of education, work hours, and range of responsibilities would command vastly higher salaries in school or business administration, or in legal or medical professions. As seminarians have entered parish ministry with greater and greater debt loads, the frustration has only grown.

Sometimes, it feels like the lever has been turned around and we are trying to lift from the short side of the fulcrum:

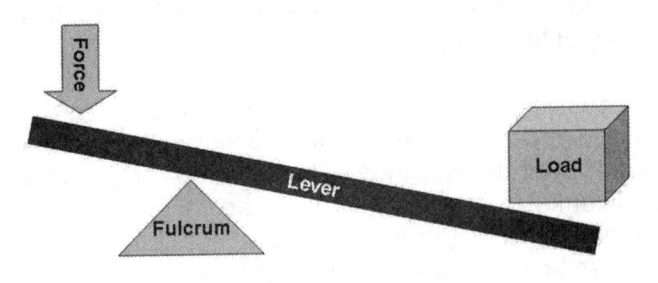

A Dysfunctional Lever

Wise and creative staffing will undoubtedly be a hallmark of thriving churches in the coming decades. For nearly a century, the church yoking model has been the popular last resort for declining churches: two or more churches that can no longer separately afford a pastor, share one. There are newer variations including larger numbers of churches sharing multiple pastors as well as other staff. The track record for these innovative experiments is mixed. Such arrangements will continue into the future, but they are clearly only one piece of the puzzle.

An approach that is both more logical and more radical begins with a question: Do we pay church workers to do tasks, primarily:
- that we *can't* do; or
- that we *don't want* to do?

Some traditions have rules that permit only clergy to preside at communion. Some tasks, like preaching, require skills, knowledge, or gifts, which we may or may not find within our volunteer pool. Some tasks, like visiting lonely widows and widowers in their homes, has primarily fallen to pastors not because of the need for special skills and training – but because no one else wanted to do it. Some churches have had a solo pastor, a part-time secretary, a part-time custodian, and a part-time organist for as long as anyone can remember. Churches that have grown beyond that formula have rarely done so in increments that precisely matched those ratios. The larger that a staff is, the more luxury that a congregation has in strategically matching needs to staffing levels. Larger staffs also have their own unique stresses, but the ability to staff strategically is a great point of leverage.

Before wrestling, once again, with the annual budget challenge of *how do we pay the pastor*, many churches would be blessed to first ask *what do we pay the pastor to do?* Don't misinterpret this as license to attempt micro-managing the work time of all church staff. Your staff members probably have a pretty good level of self-awareness about their work. Ask them these questions:
- What parts of your work need special skills, licensure, or training that most people don't have?
- What parts of your work seem to have the greatest impact in furthering the church's strategic goals?
- What parts of your work seem to have the least impact in furthering the church's strategic goals?
- What parts of your work are energizing?
- What parts of your work are draining?
- What parts of your work would be easiest for you to delegate or share with others?
- How willing are you to train and disciple others to help with some of your work?

Start the conversation now, but allow ample time to implement any changes. Some church workers have spent decades adapting themselves to a rather dysfunctional specialization of labor. They need to be extended grace and dignity as they transition out of a system that they probably weren't responsible for creating.

In military doctrine, leverage opportunities are described as force multipliers. Often, the victorious military commander has been the one that most wisely and creatively employed force multipliers to accomplish the assigned objective. God has given us some pretty big assigned objectives in the Great Commission and the Great Commandment. We won't accomplish them without lots of wisdom, creativity and leverage!

Assessment

Without consultation, plans are frustrated, But with many counselors they succeed.

- Proverbs 15:22 (NASB)

Imagine that you are a pilot flying a plane filled with passengers for a mission trip to Africa. You have planned carefully: you know the goals of the trip, the budget, even the menu for each day. Each member of the mission team has been assigned tasks that match their unique gifts. The frequent worship services will be vibrant. Each person will share daily experiences in an affinity small group. Everyone has a clearly shared set of values that unselfishly embrace evangelism. The plane takes off and midway across the Atlantic Ocean, you notice that none of the gauges in the cockpit work. You have no compass, no altimeter, no idea how much fuel you have, and only a rough idea where you are. Your GPS and radio don't work. If you can't find an airport before you run out of fuel, then none of your carefully prepared plans for the trip will matter.

If your church isn't serious about vision and goals, then developing them is a waste of time. If you are serious, then you must periodically assess where you are at in relation to those goals. On the surface, progress toward goals can seem easy to measure. If your goal is to start a new worship service, for example, you can clearly manage a checklist of all the individual tasks required to accomplish the overall goal.

Imagine that you are back in the airplane and, miraculously, your GPS starts to work. You would know where you are and what your altitude is. But, you still wouldn't know your fuel supply, oil pressure, engine temperature, the weather ahead, or dozens of other pieces of crucial information. You would be able to precisely and visually track your progress to the airport, but you might be totally unaware of a variety of dangers.

Assessment is important in ministry, because we need to remain aware of how effectively we are functioning and how the environment around us is changing. In the same way that automobiles need scheduled maintenance and people need regular health exams, so to do churches need recurring assessment.

Assessment consists of measuring and comparing. We can self-compare over time (what was my blood pressure six months ago) and we can compare to comparable groups (what is a typical blood pressure for a non-athletic man of my age). Both comparison types can be useful and dangerous. Of course, the less healthy the standard is that we compare against, the easier it is to find false confidence with whatever condition we are in. I once consulted a congregation that had declined 25% in worship attendance over the last 25 years – but they thought that their trendline was "good" since their denomination had declined by almost the same percentage. They hadn't paused to realize that they were merely rushing to disaster with lots of company!

At one of my first parishes, I was preparing my year-end parochial report – a statistical summary of the ministry year compiled for the denomination. It was a massive grid that had to be completed in triplicate. Some of the questions made sense, some required guessing, and some were clearly designed only to collect marketing data for the denominational publishing house. As I prepared to tackle this paperwork beast, I started to sift through our local attendance records. I was shocked by the monthly variation. In particular, I was surprised to learn that a recent month had shown a 20% attendance drop from the month before. As I thought back to those two months, I just couldn't imagine why such a drop occurred and how I could have failed to notice.

The attendance pattern mystery was solved when I described my puzzlement to a few lay leaders. Ushers serve one month at a time at that church and one of the usher leaders didn't think that children should be counted. So, everyone was counted eleven months per year. But during one month, only adults were counted. Since children represented about twenty percent of our attendance, there had been no actual attendance decline.

It was Mark Twain who popularized the famous phrase about three kinds of lies: "lies, damn lies, and statistics." Measuring ministry is always difficult, but even more so if the underlying measurements have no clear definition. Even the most basic measurable elements of ministry can be more subjective than we realize. Every church should track some basic data from year-to-year and every church should take the effort to insure continuity in collecting and storing that information. The following are some essentials that every church would benefit from tracking consistently year-to-year:

- **Attendance:** Average Weekly Worship attendance is a key variable. Average Weekly Sunday School attendance is also valuable.

- **Membership Cause of Change:** Many churches do not measure the components of this variable annually, but they are missing out on very important patterns. All new members should be subcategorized in groups like: transfer from a local church, transfer from a distant church, new adult Christian, and infants born to members. Likewise, membership losses should be subcategorized by type: death, transfer to a local church, transfer to a distant church, and inactivity.

- **Finances:** How much was contributed for capital, missions, general fund, and undesignated? How much was spent for capital, missions, and general fund?

With these basic data sets you can create meaningful trend reports over time.

Do-it-yourself trendline analysis is a great tool for every church, but it offers insight to only a tiny slice of the complex systems that make up your church. Think of it like a silhouette or shadow image of your body. A silhouette can yield clues about posture, height, and girth – but it is of little value in measuring pulse or respiration. An X-ray, MRI, and blood tests would reveal different sorts of information – all of which would collectively contribute to a more accurate description of your health.

You may be aware that medical doctors and automotive mechanics each use stethoscopes as diagnostic tools. Beyond that one similarity though, doctors and mechanics use very different tools specialized for their respective work. Churches also require uniquely specialized diagnostic tools.

For decades now, places like Hartford Seminary and Fuller Seminary have contributed research from different perspectives about how churches function. Organizations like the Great Commission Research Network (formerly the ASCG) have allowed scholars and practitioners to trade insights. Various church assessment tools sprang from this rich cross-pollination of theologies and methodologies. All of the tools available today owe some debt to a range of work which preceded all current efforts. Today, we can couple the power of the relational database with the wisdom and insights of a broad range of faithful servants of the Gospel.

Over a cup of coffee, I would be happy to explain why my *Glass Cockpit* is special. But, the reality is that there are many good assessment tools and that their differing perspectives are a blessing for churches. Kent Hunter's *Church Vitality Profile* has been a blessing for many churches, as has Schwarz's *NCD* and Willow Creek's *Reveal*. There is no singular magic test that yields all possible insights about every church. Churches that do one assessment annually and rotate amongst the *Glass Cockpit,* the *Church Vitality Profile, NCD,* and *Reveal* will benefit both from the differing perspectives and the ability to observe long-term trends with each instrument.

Imagine that you are back in the cockpit of your jet on the way to Africa. Most of the gauges still don't work, but a helpful passenger has crawled into a space beneath the cockpit and found a way to access some crude information. She relays the news that a particular tank is almost completely empty – but she doesn't know the contents of the tank or how full it is supposed to be. Maybe that tank is supposed to be mostly empty. Maybe the critical indication isn't the fullness of the tank, but the color or viscosity of the fluid. Appropriate knowledge in the field is necessary to make sense out of what is observed. The observable patterns which churches find through assessment must be matched with useful knowledge.

A client church was concerned when I first shared the results of their assessment. The leaders gathered around the conference table were anxious and unhappy to hear that 30% of their congregation never read their Bibles. What they had yet to hear me explain was that more than 30% of the congregation's respondents were relatively new Christians. When we looked at the subtle detail of the patterns, we could see that Bible usage patterns were very good among all groups that had been at the church for more than a year. Reaching the unchurched and aiding members in growing spiritually were two highly valued goals at that congregation. What the data patterns showed was that they were actually doing a good job of pursuing both goals, but they needed someone who understood their data and ministry to make sense of it all.

Good ministry consultants make those connections for churches and offer clear guidance for making the minor adjustments that are necessary to get from where you are to where you want to be. Good consultants bring specialized knowledge of the field along with objective and subjective assessment skills. If they are a ministry expert but aren't able to discern the unique realities of your context, then go listen to them at a conference. If they are expert at widget manufacturing and assessment, then don't seek their advice unless you plan to stop doing ministry and start building widgets.

Churches are neither clubs nor businesses. There are powerful tools and strategies that we can very selectively borrow from experiences in those two arenas, but selectivity is crucial. The closest professional analogy for ministry is the growing field of non-profit administration, but even among other non-profits churches are quite unique. We shouldn't even be lumped together with other religious groups – though there is a dangerous trend of viewing concepts like interim ministry as universal to all churches, mosques, and synagogues.

Churches are the Body of Christ. No other type of organization holds that unique identity. Churches need assessment tools and consulting expertise that is not merely Christ-tolerant or Christ-optional, but that is focused on Christ.

Money

As soon as Hezekiah's orders had gone out, the Israelites responded generously: firstfruits of the grain harvest, new wine, oil, honey—everything they grew. They didn't hold back, turning over a tithe of everything. They also brought in a tithe of their cattle, sheep, and anything else they owned that had been dedicated to God. Everything was sorted and piled in mounds.

– 2 Chronicles 31:5-6 (MSG)

Churches can exist in barter economies. Churches can exist and even thrive in settings of dire poverty with miniscule financial resources. For most churches though, money plays a significant role in how and what we get done. Therefore, how we receive, manage, and expend funds is a significant responsibility of ministry leaders.

Generally, people entrust their offerings to a church motivated by some combination of five factors:
- **Vision**: People can be compellingly inspired to support a vision for ministry because they want to see that vision fulfilled.
- **Fear**: Desperation to keep a church open can create a powerful sense of necessity.
- **Pride**: That engraved brass nameplate affixed to the stained glass window really strokes the ego of some.
- **Scripture**: The 10% tithe, the teaching about the widow's mite, and many other passages inspire those who recognize the authority of scripture in matters of daily life.
- **Tax deductibility**: Very few people give solely for this reason, but it can change the amount that people perceive that they are able to give.

Guilt, gratitude, and peer pressure combine in powerful ways with the factors listed. All these variables interact in ways that are sometimes complimentary and sometimes in tension. An emerging trend that affects a small percentage of giving is the decision by some who honor the 10% tithe but feel compelled to split their offering between their local church and other ministries, motivated by: doctrinal disputes, personality conflicts, perceived need, lack of trust, or other reasons. So, even if your members all tithe, it is still necessary to make the case for entrusting that tithe to your congregation.

Decades ago, a somewhat popular rule-of-thumb arose that churches should always be in debt. The premise of the theory was that church members give more when congregations have debt. There was a fairly broad pool of data and experience that confirmed this correlation. Although debt and giving had a clear relationship, it was not a causal relationship. Vision inspired the giving to pay for the building that was financed with debt. Vision, not debt, was the causal factor. Debt is a powerful financial tool, but not a great motivator. That is why capital campaigns tend to be easier at the start of a building project than they are ten years later when the paint has started to peel, but a sizable mortgage remains. Debt is useful, but not inspirational.

Good money-handling procedures engender trust and are necessary as a matter of good managerial stewardship. Every church should be attentive to these basics:

- **Multiple Counters:** No single individual or household should ever handle the offering. All counters should be trained and in some type of rotation so that different counters are paired weekly.
- **Separation:** People who handle money coming into the church should not be involved with money being expended. Ideally, there is also separation between check-writing and check-signing.
- **Audit:** Every church should have an internal audit every year. Occasional external audits are highly desirable and can be a service "traded" between volunteers at two different congregations.
- **Term Limits:** Having a treasurer serve for decades is unsafe because of risk and unwise because it tends to create unhealthy dependence. The crucial exception is that many churches have consolidated the accounting and check-writing tasks to a single position, but isolate the person doing that work from any check-signing authority.

- **Clear procedures:** The offering count, the recording of contributions, the approval of payments, the generation and signing of checks, the process for balance transfers and reconciliation, the budget process, and the audit should all be accurately described by a thorough set of procedures that are reviewed annually at the time of the audit.
- **Church Address:** Every bank statement and church authorized credit card statement should be sent only to the church address. Every account in the congregation's name should be reviewed every year at the time of the audit. Dormant accounts should be closed.
- **Paper Trail:** Every expenditure should have supporting documentation that is retained. Records that are computerized should be regularly backed-up with offsite storage.

The above list is a brief and crude summary of a much broader topic. Sadly, many congregations still are not in compliance with even this minimal level of procedural safety. Your insurance carrier probably has free guidelines available in greater detail. *The Complete Handbook of Church Accounting* by Manfred Holck (Senior & Junior) is over three decades old, but still probably one of the best overall guides. Computer accounting software has dramatically eased the burden on church treasurers and, simultaneously, boosted the quality and usefulness of reports available to leaders.

A good church accounting system should be invoice-driven and based on an approved budget. Your system should clearly delineate who has authority to authorize expenditures, for what amounts, and for which budget categories.

Budgeting can be a curious mix of boring drudgery, exciting vision clarification, power politics, and guesswork. Incremental budgeting (starting with last year's budget and modestly adjusting each category slightly up or down) is very common and very dangerous. It is common because it is the easiest, quickest, and most practical way to accomplish a necessary task. It is dangerous because it assumes that next year should mostly look like this year. Ideally, we want next year to look more like God's vision that we have discerned for our future. There are lots of creative ways to keep the budgeting process fresh and open without making the budget a black hole that sucks in all available leadership time and energy. If ministry leaders have a clear sense about priorities 12 and 24 months into the future, then budgeting is likely to focus more on the future than the past.

A common money concern in churches is the secrecy of individual member donation records. There are widely divergent views on this point, both among pastors and laity. If giving records are unavailable to the pastor, then the pastor should also be blindfolded when preaching and administering sacraments. Our giving is one dimension among many of our overall spiritual health, as are worship attendance and receiving Holy Communion. If you honestly think that your pastor is too spiritually shallow to deal with this information, then a good discussion following the pattern of Matthew 18 needs to take place. If you think that all pastors are too spiritually shallow to deal with this information, then there are probably some long established unhealthy stewardship attitudes that need adjusting at your church.

This aversion to money issues in the church is part of a larger dynamic of deep-rooted but unscriptural views about money that have leaked from the culture to the church. Look through your Bible and see how often money is discussed. It is a very common and frequently recurring topic. Our individual stewardship of everything entrusted to us by God is something that we should, out of love and concern, help one another to be prepared to ultimately account for to God. As communities of faith, we are obligated to model scripturally healthy attitudes about money.

If a little brass nameplate glued to the baptismal font helps to raise funds to buy the font, does that offset Matthew 6:1? Perhaps, but how many churches really wrestle with the broad implications of such policy issues? There are solid arguments on both sides of a variety of church money issues. Just be sure that scriptural attitudes are given a voice in your discussions. Don't affirm unscriptural values about money out of frustration to secure funds in the short-run. Remember, our pragmatic decisions can have eternal consequences!

Good managerial stewardship is one way that we model healthy scriptural attitudes. Penny wise and pound foolish management makes the church look bad. Before saving a few hundred dollars buying inkjet instead of laser printers, look at the lifetime cost of ink versus toner. Think about the hourly cost of employing your staff, before deciding that a fast internet connection is too expensive. Think about all these things, but don't obsess. Money is a tool to advance ministry, not vice versa. If you are spending more time talking about money than ministry, then the tail is wagging the dog. Deal wisely with money, but focus on ministry.

Epilogue

I pray that this book will equip church leaders to discern and adopt the right strategies for implementing the right changes for the future. I am a strong proponent of *non-reckless innovation*. Every church needs to innovate, but no church needs every innovation. I was able to parrot the phrase "choose your battles" long before I really started to incorporate that reality into my ministry leadership.

I pray that you won't use this book as a club. We should be slow to malign others for repeating unhealthy ministry leadership patterns if no one has taught them a better way.

I pray that you will realize how condensed this overview is. Pruning this book down to a manageable size has been painful. Every chapter could easily have been accompanied by a chapter of *Yes But*, expanding on many exceptions and contradictions. Many times, a list of 5 key variables could have been expanded to 7 or 12, but for the sake of brevity was condensed. Some important topics were left out, like: assimilation, dynamics of congregational size, role of the denomination, conflict resolution, and spiritual formation. A whole chapter could be devoted to ministry lingo and another to the influence of key individuals like Arn, McGavran, Gibbs, Wagner, Schaller, Towns, Hybels, and Warren.

I pray that you have experienced the three elements of primer that this book endeavors to offer: to be a basic instructional text, to provide a preparatory coat, and to ignite powerful change. It is up to you to learn more, to add layers of experience, and to spark wise and faithful change in your church.

I pray that you are primed!

About the Author

The Rev. Dr. Brad Miller, founder of ChurchTech, has over 20 years of experience working to enhance ministry with the aid of analytic tools and technology. He is passionate about helping churches to grow in healthy ways. He was a parish pastor in the ELCA for 17 years and is now a pastor in the LCMC. He has served congregations in a variety of different contexts: urban & rural, large & small. His experience includes: church construction, capital appeals, church planting, and conflict resolution. He is a trained Intentional Interim Minister.

Starting in 1990 he began to organize and conduct ecumenical conferences and seminars on ministry and technology. He has also been a presenter on those same topics at seminars organized by others (like *Christian Computing Magazine*). Dr. Miller has been a featured presenter at conferences and seminars throughout the U.S. and abroad.

He was the developer of the *Glass Cockpit* church health and growth assessment tool, as well as various templates and tools for use with software for churches.

Dr. Miller received his B.S. In Public Affairs from Indiana University in 1987. He received his M. Div. From Wartburg Theological Seminary in 1992 and was ordained as a pastor that same year. Under the mentorship of Dr. Kent Hunter, he was trained as an Associate Church Doctor. He earned his D.Min. from Agape Seminary in 2006.

When not consulting churches, Dr. Miller is available to speak at ministry leadership events and particularly looks forward to opportunities to teach church leaders in Africa.

His wife, Pam Schroeder, is also a pastor, currently serving as a Hospice Chaplain. They reside in Des Moines, Iowa and have two teenage children.

Are you interested in…

…more copies of this book?

…audio or large print versions of this book?

…the *Glass Cockpit* ministry assessment tool?

…booking Dr. Miller for a speaking engagement?

…a workshop on 8D Leadership?

… scheduling a consultation?

…some FREE resources?

For all of the above and more, please visit:

www.churchtech.com